ASTON MARTIN
DB2, DB2/4 & DB3

In Detail

ASTON MARTIN
DB2, DB2/4 & DB3

In Detail

1950-59

BY NICK WALKER

Herridge & Sons

Published in 2004 by
Herridge & Sons Ltd
Lower Forda, Shebbear,
Beaworthy, Devon EX21 5SY

Reprinted 2012, 2018

Designed by Ray Leaning
Special photography by Simon Clay

ISBN 978-0-9541063-3-1
Printed in China

Picture Acknowledgments
The author and the publisher are grateful to the
following for supplying photographs:

Aston Martin Heritage Trust, Neill Bruce, Brian Joscelyne,
Neil Murray, Swiss Car Register, David Wright.

Contents

Introduction

The DB2 series of Aston Martins, and their immediate predecessor which has become known as the DB1, were the first models to be made after the Second World War. Like many designs at that time, they went through a long gestation period. The whole industry, in trying to restart production, faced not just a buying public conditioned to austerity after six years of war, but a continuation of rationing and controls imposed by a government which was trying to steer the economy in a fixed direction. The need to keep a tight grip on foreign exchange was paramount, and to keep this flowing in there was a huge campaign to promote exports. Only those firms which were exporting a large proportion of their output received a steel allocation; but if you were developing a new product which was not yet on the market you had no exports and therefore did not qualify for an allocation. Aston Martin were one of many firms trying to fight their way out of that vicious circle, and it was only when they were able to use the resources of the David Brown group that progress speeded up.

Once a few cars had been produced, the circle became a virtuous one. The first works cars took part in competition from the beginning, with

notable success. This became the platform for a sales drive both in the United States and throughout Europe, and the orders started to flow in. Those early years of the DB2 were exciting times; the cars which you could see and buy in the showroom were (ostensibly) identical to the ones which were winning at Silverstone and Le Mans. This sporting bias was reflected in the clientele, where famous names such as Phil Hill and Briggs Cunningham were buying the cars with the sole intention of racing them.

Soon, however, there was a change, and there was no going back. Whereas previously the organisers of sports car races such as the Le Mans 24-Hours had insisted on cars being production models, the introduction of a "sports prototype" class soon saw a split opening up between production and racing cars. Aston Martin, convinced of the value of competition in promoting sales, were forced down this route, which resulted in the DB3 sports-racing cars and their successors. Nominally they were available to the public, but precious few were bought for any purpose other than racing. This left the DB2 to evolve into more of a continental tourer (the "GT" tag had yet to be invented), albeit one with outstanding performance and carrying an enormous sporting heritage.

Thereafter the DB2 models were understandably eclipsed by the glamorous supercars which followed: DB4/5/6, DBS, V8 and so on. For a time, indeed, these early postwar cars with their comparatively small six-cylinder engines were not as eagerly sought after by those Aston Martin enthusiasts who wanted a classic model. In recent years, however, their purity of design and their sheer value for money have brought them sharply back into favour. Not only are there specific racing classes for them, but the owner who has bought one merely for the pleasure of driving it at weekends finds that he has acquired a very practical machine which can often carry the whole family.

This book is at once a tribute to these splendid cars and an introduction to them. For those who

DB2 in its sporting heyday - the Wisdom/Nockolds car during the 1952 Alpine Rally.

XVᵐᵉ RALLYE INTERNATIONAL DES ALPES
CRITERIUM DE LA MONTAGNE DU 11 AU 17 JUILLET 1952

Stirling Moss in classic pose drifting a DB3S.

are already familiar with the range, the book will – I hope – provide a convenient repository of facts, figures and history between one set of covers. For those who do not yet possess detailed knowledge of the cars, but who are attracted to them, it is my modest hope that the book will answer their immediate questions and even, perhaps, persuade them to consider ownership. As well as giving some background on the Aston Martin company, it covers all those models produced after World War Two up to and including the move from Feltham to Newport Pagnell. Since the book is aimed at those who are going to use the cars on the road it includes the DB3 and DB3S models but not the DBR1, which was an out-and-out racer with no pretence to be road-legal.

To write about such marvellous cars is a pleasure in itself, and it has been made more so by the help and cooperation I have received on all sides. Outstanding in this respect has been the Aston Martin Owners' Club and their alter ego, the Aston Martin Heritage Trust. Their combined headquarters – housed in a beautiful converted barn, and worth a visit in its own right – contains priceless archive material, which the Trust made available to me. Neil Murray, trustee extraordinaire, gave up numerous mornings to provide his help, and is himself a mine of information; I am particularly grateful to him for agreeing to read through the text. This is not to imply that any mistakes can be laid at his door. If they do arise they are mine alone and I can only apologise – and ask that readers let me know, so that the errors can be corrected at an appropriate time.

I am also very appreciative of the cooperation I received from every one of the owners who kindly made their cars available to be photographed. One of these prefers to remain anonymous, but the others are Carl Bates, Mike Jankowski, Ian MacGregor and Richard Royle; many thanks to you all. On a wider front – and thanks to the facilities of the Vintage Sports-Car Club library – I have been able to draw on the fund of wisdom which already exists. I have tried to use contemporary reports wherever possible, but other sources to which I am indebted are Aston Martin: The Story of a Sports Car (Hunter/Ellis/Coram), Aston Martin and Lagonda: Six-Cylinder DB Models (Whyte), Racing with DB Aston Martins (Nixon/Wyer) and Aston Martin: The Compleat Car (Archer et al).

Supreme elegance: DB2/4 in an appropriate setting.

Chapter One

Aston Martin between the wars

The origins of the first Aston Martin go back to before the First World War. Lionel Martin and Robert Bamford were friends from their youth, when they were involved in the sport of cycle road-racing at the beginning of the twentieth century. As with so many young men at that time, their interest strayed from pedals to the internal combustion engine, and it was not long before Martin acquired a motorcycle and then turned his thoughts towards cars. As it happens it was Bamford who was the apprentice-trained engineer, although Martin seems to have had an instinctive feeling for machinery even though he lacked the training. By 1912 the two had set up in business as motor engineers in the South Kensington area of London, trading as Bamford & Martin. As a partnership the two fitted together well: Bamford had the technical knowledge, and Martin, described as "a big, intelligent, extremely well-mannered Etonian", was ideal as the front-man.

The next obvious step was to become authorised dealers for a respected make of car, and the pair's choice fell on Singer. At that time Singer had a well-established reputation as a "big car in miniature" which had done well in trials, and this was a formula which appealed particularly to Martin. When the firm had been officially appointed agents for south-east England the two partners decided to form it into a limited company, and this took place officially on 15 June 1913. Martin's thoughts seem to have turned immediately towards sporting activities for these cars. However, although there were plenty of events for which light cars were eligible, there were very few out-and-out sports cars in this class. The 10hp Singer, good as it was, certainly did not qualify with its 40mph maximum. Martin therefore set about modifying his personal Singer to make it more competitive, eventually doubling the car's maximum speed and achieving great success in speed trials and hill-climbs.

Inevitably this brought in more business from customers who wanted their own Singers modified in a similar manner. Martin realised that there was an opportunity for someone who could produce what he called a "British-built fast touring car", but at the same time he realised that the facilities available at Bamford & Martin Ltd were wholly unsuited

Lionel Martin, left, and Robert Bamford.

"Coal Scuttle", the first Aston Martin, with works foreman Jack Addis driving.

to the production of cars from scratch. He decided that the firm would instead assemble a car from proprietary components, and began by casting around for a suitable engine. This turned out to be a four-cylinder sidevalve design from Coventry Simplex, with the head cast integral with the block, and a bore and stroke of 66.5 x 100mm giving a capacity of 1389cc. Chassis components were ordered at the same time, but the engine arrived first, and in order to test it Martin installed it in a chassis from a 1908 Isotta-Fraschini. His own chassis, when it finally arrived, was notable for having three-quarter elliptic springs at the rear, with more conventional semi-elliptics at the front. Thus was the first Aston Martin born, the name coming from the Aston Clinton hill-climb where Martin had scored some successes with his Singer.

Although Martin entered the new car for a few events, war had already broken out and there could be little further development work until hostilities ceased, especially as Bamford had gone off to the war. However, the car, known as "Coal Scuttle" because of the shape of its open bodywork, was used continuously on the road throughout the period, which can only have provided much useful experience. In the immediate postwar period it achieved some success in competition, but there was little progress in getting the model into production. Partly this was because by that time Bamford had lost interest in the business and resigned from the company; in his place as director came Mrs (Katherine) Martin. At about the same time the firm moved to larger premises in West Kensington.

Although the Aston Martin was listed in the motoring press as available for sale during 1920, there was no move to production that year. The reason was a major redesign of the whole car, including the engine, this latter being the work of the Coventry Simplex designer himself, H V Robb. The stroke was increased to 107mm, bringing capacity up to 1486cc – conveniently near the limit of the 1500cc class. There were three main bearings rather than two, timing gears instead of a chain, and a more sophisticated lubrication system. The chassis was improved in a number of respects, including semi-elliptic springs all round. In this form the car was finally offered to the public early in 1921, at the exalted prices of £500 for a chassis or £650 for a complete car. The following year the specification was further improved by the addition of front-wheel brakes. Three experimental chassis had been built, and a production run of 100 was envisaged – optimistically, as things turned out.

Martin immediately concentrated on publicising the car through competition, and entered a cut-down experimental chassis with a narrow body, known throughout its long life as "Bunny", in as many events as possible. Although he achieved some success he had already realised that the sidevalve engine had reached the end of its development, and accordingly he commissioned Robb to produce a new overhead-camshaft 16-valve engine. The project was encouraged, and possibly part-financed, by the ebullient Count Zborowski (of Chitty-Bang-Bang fame), who wanted a light car which he could drive in the

Clive Gallop in "Bunny" at Brooklands, after the car's record-breaking 18-hour run.

TT1, later to become known as "Green Pea", being prepared at the West London factory for the 1922 Tourist Trophy.

new 200-mile race at Brooklands in October 1921. The engine was completed just in time, but in the race it could only bring the Count home in tenth place. Particularly galling was that Bunny came in ahead, in ninth place; the truth was that the new engine's power – about 40bhp – was no more than that of the sidevalve.

During the winter of 1921-22 Bunny was used for record attempts at Brooklands, and achieved new world records in the 15- to 19-hour classes. In the meantime, at Zborowski's insistence, the company developed a new version of the Robb engine, this time with twin overhead camshafts. Although bore and stroke were changed, to 63 x 112mm, the resulting capacity was the same at 1486cc. Its improved shape of combustion chamber lifted power output considerably, to some 55bhp, and gave the car a maximum speed of 90mph. Two such cars were entered for the 1922 French Grand Prix at Strasbourg, but both retired with magneto problems. The dohc cars were later campaigned with some success by Zborowski and others, and a production version, the Super Sports, was eventu-·ally offered to the public. However there were very few sales until 1923, and even then not enough to ensure the viability of the business.

During the winter of 1923-24 it became obvious that Bamford & Martin Ltd were in financial trouble; Martin's efforts in gaining publicity through competition had not paid off in sufficient sales. Thus in July 1924 control of the business passed to Lady Charnwood, who became a director along with her son, the Hon John Benson.

He immediately set about designing an eight-valve, twin overhead camshaft engine, which was intended for the 200-mile race but was never used. The company struggled on through 1925, and even took a stand at that year's London Motor Show, but all the time against a background of insufficient finance. The Show produced numerous enquiries but not many orders, and within a week of its closing the company went into receivership. This spelt the end of Lionel Martin's connection with the company, and for a time it looked as if the Aston Martin name would disappear as well.

The receiver, a Mr Arthur Whale, had approaches from several possible buyers, including Vauxhall Motors, but no offer materialised for some time. Eventually, after nearly a year had elapsed, a deal was done with the Birmingham firm of Renwick & Bertelli. In October 1926 a new company, Aston Martin Motors Ltd, was formed, its directors being Lord Charnwood, the Hon John Benson, A C Bertelli and W S Renwick. Of the two new directors, there is no doubt that the dominant personality was August Cesare ("Bert") Bertelli. Having spent many of his early years in England, he had joined the Fiat company in Turin for a time, his experience there including acting as riding mechanic to the great Felice Nazzaro. He returned to England after the end of World War I and became general manager of (and frequent works driver for) the Enfield-Allday car company; it was here that he met Renwick, who was works manager. When the Enfield-Allday concern failed in 1922, Bertelli went to work for Woolf Barnato. Then in 1924 he and Renwick set up in business together with the intention of manufacturing their own car. At the time that the Aston Martin business attracted their attention they had built a prototype, the main interest lying in its engine, which had an advanced design of cylinder head. Their design draughtsman was Claude Hill, whom they brought with them into the Aston Martin company and who would have a profound impact on future models for more than 20 years.

The new firm set up in Feltham, on the western edge of London, the West Kensington premises being retained initially as a service depot. The new buildings bordered Hanworth Air Park, and had until then been used by Citröen as their British assembly plant. The Renwick & Bertelli business also moved there, and soon there was a complete manufacturing set-up covering machine and assembly shops, body-building and drawing office. The body-building department was to be run separately by Bert Bertelli's brother Enrico (known as Harry). All attention was now focussed on producing a completely new car under the Aston Martin name, and it duly appeared at the 1927 Motor Show. It incorporated the Renwick & Bertelli engine, which was of 1488cc capacity with a bore and stroke of 69 x 99mm and of course used the

A 1923 sidevalve Aston Martin, still going strong when this picture was taken in 1946.

An International sportsmans coupé, chassis S49, which was probably the 1930 Olympia Show car.

special patented head. This combined inclined valves, operated from a single overhead camshaft, with a Ricardo-style wedge-shaped combustion chamber, promising added turbulence and therefore much improved mixture control. Other features of the engine included three main bearings, double valve springs and a cooling system which was pump-driven for the head and thermosyphon for the block.

The chassis was all new and included worm-gear final drive (from the David Brown company of Huddersfield). It was offered in long (9ft 6in/2895mm) or short (8ft 6in/2590mm) forms, the intention being to produce saloons and tourers on the longer version and a sports model on the shorter one. The short chassis was underslung at the rear and strengthened, and its engine had twin carburettors and a higher compression ratio. Chassis prices were lower than for the outgoing Bamford & Martin models, at £465 and £495 for long and short respectively.

Like Lionel Martin, Bertelli believed in competition as a means both of improving his cars and of giving them wide publicity. He therefore prepared two cars for the 1928 Le Mans, with even shorter chassis than the standard Sports. Engine improvements included the dry-sump lubrication with the

oil reservoir slung between the front dumb-irons – a prominent recognition point of these and future models. This feature allowed the engines to be set lower in the chassis and gave a lower bonnet and radiator line; the radiator, incidentally, was the first to carry the now-famous winged Aston Martin badge. Power output was 56bhp at 4250rpm. The cars did not distinguish themselves in the race, both having to retire, but one did sufficiently well to be awarded the prize for the fastest 1½-litre car in the first 20 laps.

In the light of the Le Mans experience Bertelli decided that the company's time would be better spent in improving the standard models rather than indulging in more competition immediately. Even so, the performance of the new dry-sump engine had been sufficiently encouraging for it to be offered as an alternative power unit on the Sports chassis; in this form the car was described as the International Sports, forever afterwards to be known amongst Aston Martin cognoscenti as the International. Although it cost little more than the standard Sports – £598 with two-seater body, as against £575 – it offered considerably better performance, with the motoring journals achieving maximum speeds between 80 and 84mph in their road tests. For the 1929 season there was the

prospect of the new Double-Twelve race at Brooklands, involving two sessions of 12 hours each on successive days, with the cars locked up during the intervening night. This was more attractive than the trek to Le Mans, and the company entered two cars with their weight reduced wherever possible. One car had to retire, but the other, driven by Bertelli and his works foreman Jack Bezzant, finished fifth overall and third in its class.

Further minor modifications were made in time for that year's Motor Show, which must have impressed certain key people as immediately afterwards there was yet another financial reconstruction, with new directors arriving. A new company, Aston Martin Ltd, took over the assets of both Aston Martin Motors and Renwick & Bertelli, and one of its board members was the highly regarded Percy Kidner, formerly joint chairman of Vauxhall Motors. In the 1930 season one of the works cars achieved a fourth place in the Double-Twelve race, and in 1931 there were works entries for both this race and Le Mans, where Bertelli managed fifth overall. However the effect of the Depression on sales meant that finance was a perpetual struggle, and it was not long before there were further changes at the top of the company.

During 1931 both the Charnwood family and Renwick severed their connection with the company, and new directors came and went. For a period H J Aldington of AFN Ltd, makers of the Frazer Nash, helped to finance the company, and in return he handled Aston Martin sales from his Isleworth headquarters. This arrangement did not last, and Kensington-Moir & Straker Ltd became the London agents, with Nigel Holder and Reginald Straker of that company becoming board members. However, towards the end of the year the London agency passed to Jack Olding & Co Ltd. Some idea of the company's parlous financial state can be gauged from their sales record: from the re-start of production in late 1927 to the end of 1931 only some 130 cars had been sold.

There was clearly a pressing need to keep prices down, which meant reducing costs of production. Bertelli therefore put in hand a redesign using proprietary components wherever possible, while endeavouring not to destroy the car's character. Even this project brought the need for further financing, and for 1932 this came from the company's southern counties distributor, L Prideaux Brune, who of course joined the board of directors. Bertelli's second series New International used a new, cheaper chassis and a Laycock gearbox in

Another Show car, this time the 1932 Olympia. Fabric-covered bodies had given way to metal panels.

Kitty Brunell, a keen competitor in the 1930s, with Gordon Sutherland and the red Le Mans model which she drove in the 1933 Scottish Rally.

"Bert" Bertelli (in the white overalls) with Sammy Davis (right) at Le Mans in 1933.

unit with the engine, while the worm-drive rear axle was replaced by an ENV spiral-bevel unit. Other improvements included a move from the Perrot front braking system to cable operation. The cost reduction measures had worked, and the new car in 2/4-seater form was priced at £475, a full £120 less than the outgoing model.

For Le Mans that year the works cars used an engine with a modified head producing 70bhp at 5000rpm and a maximum speed approaching 90mph. The result was a triumph for the marque, with two cars finishing fifth and seventh overall. The seventh-place car – Bertelli's, which had quali-

fied the previous year – won the Biennial Cup for the best performance over two years. This inspired the company to develop a new Le Mans model for the Motor Show, incorporating the special features of the works cars including their trademark lower radiators. Business up to then had been very thin, with Harry Bertelli's bodywork department even accepting work on other makes of chassis. Furthermore the Le Mans model made the International look staid and slow by comparison, and orders for it slowed to the point where it was dropped from the catalogue. After the Show the expected flow of orders for the Le Mans model began, but not quickly enough for Prideaux Brune, who decided that he wanted to sell his investment in the company (although he remained very much involved as distributor for London and the southern counties).

In his place came yet another investor, who this time would remain for a considerable period and who would prove to be a profound influence for the company's good. This was Sir Arthur Sutherland, who had made his fortune in shipping, and whose son, R Gordon Sutherland, came into the business at the same time and joined the board. The younger Sutherland was immediately appointed joint managing director alongside Bertelli, signalling that he intended to take an active part in the day-to-day affairs of the company, if only to protect the family investment. Someone of Gordon Sutherland's tender age – he was only 24 – could easily have provoked either resentment or contempt in the existing management, and it is to his credit that he seems to have avoided both. For one thing he had received a sound engineering training, together with car industry experience in the design department of the Alvis company. More importantly, he demonstrated a flair for the commercial side of the business, and this Bertelli seems to have welcomed in that it allowed him to concentrate on technical matters.

The Sutherlands' first year, 1933, saw some greatly improved results. The main seller was now the Le Mans with the 2/4-seater body, and later in the year it was joined by the Le Mans Special with a longer wheelbase and a full four-seater body. The motoring press queued up to borrow demonstrators for road-testing, and were universal in their praise. Maximum speeds in those days of 85-86mph (for the 2/4-seater) or 82mph (for the larger car) were outstanding for a 1½-litre car at the time, and the buying public were also impressed. By the end of the year some 105 cars had been sold – twice the number of any previous year. Sporting activities were confined to Le Mans, using the previous season's cars, and with further success: the leading Aston Martin finished fifth overall and second in the Biennial Cup.

There were no major changes in the specification of the Le Mans model for the 1933 Motor Show, but 1934 saw the introduction of the Mark II version, which had numerous minor revisions. Visually the biggest differences were a flat-topped scuttle and the use of thermostatically-controlled radiator shutters in place of the previous wire-mesh grille. Later in the year the engine was uprated with a new camshaft, modified head and stiffer, fully balanced crankshaft, resulting in an increase in power to 73bhp at 4750rpm. In addition to the polished radiator shutters, there was evidence of other cosmetic changes beloved of car salesmen of the time, such as huge quick-action filler caps and a chromium-plated cap over the hole for the starting-handle. The hood was now fitted outside the body to give more room at the back. On the long-wheelbase chassis the four-seater was joined by a good-looking sports saloon.

The team cars for that year were once again aimed primarily at Le Mans, and also the Tourist Trophy in Ulster. Engine revisions included a 9:1 compression ratio, higher-lift camshafts and an improved Laystall crankshaft with larger main bearings. The chassis were liberally drilled to reduce weight, and as an offering to the gods Bertelli, a superstitious individual, omitted the number 13 from the run of chassis numbers. It was to no avail: the Le Mans result was disastrous, all three cars having to retire (although one had held second

The Aston Martin team for the 1935 Le Mans.

A Two-Litre Speed Model.

A 15/98 short-chassis 2/4-seater open sports.

place for many hours). For the TT, therefore, Bertelli decided on one final throw of the dice and changed the cars' livery from British racing green to the red of his native Italy. At the same time he had to rebuild the cars completely with standard chassis, as the lightened versions were not eligible. The change of colour seems to have worked, as the cars finished third, fifth and seventh overall, came first and second in their class, and also won the team prize.

Bertelli and Sutherland judged this success noteworthy enough to justify the launch of a new model in its honour. Thus was born the Ulster,

probably the best known and most sought after of all the pre-1939 Aston Martins, which was sold with a guaranteed maximum of 100mph. It was in effect a replica of the works cars, from the 80bhp engine down to the two-seater body with the spare wheel carried horizontally in the tail. Ulster drivers, it was decided, had no need of chromium plate, preferring to avoid reflections in their eyes, so nearly all the bright parts of the Mark II were painted instead; the radiator shutters went, replaced by a mesh grille. The left-hand side of the instrument panel was an impressive mass of switchgear, since all the electrical components,

This is a 1938 15/98 short-chassis drophead coupe. It was a works demonstrator and Autocar *road-test car.*

including magneto and fuel pumps, were separately wired and fused.

Only 21 Ulster models were built – not surprisingly considering that they were priced at £750 compared with £610 for the Mark II 2/4 seater. Nevertheless they had a disproportionate impact on the company's image, and no doubt encouraged Sutherland to agree to a works team again for the 1935 season. Further engine work raised the output to 85bhp at 5250rpm, and the radiator was lowered once more to give a downward sloping bonnet line. After his 1934 experience Bertelli could not resist the temptation to paint the cars red. Although the works cars were not involved, the season opened with the good news that a private entry had won its class in the Mille Miglia. (This achievement so surprised the Italian officials that they insisted on the engine being dismantled and measured.) The main effort once again went towards Le Mans, particularly as there was a possibility of winning the Biennial Cup, and fortunately this is exactly what happened. The same car also won its class and came third overall.

In the Tourist Trophy the cars put up a reasonable showing. There was trouble early on with flexible oil-pipes splitting, but two cars survived to

"Donald Duck", the first experimental spaceframe car and predecessor to "Atom".

the finish, gaining fourth and fifth places. Since the third car had survived to within two laps of the finish it also qualified, and so the three cars won the team award. However, this last event of 1935 also marked the last time for 13 years that a works team would appear. Sutherland had become increasingly concerned at the cost of taking part in high-level competition, but had agreed to a works entry in the 1936 Le Mans. In the end matters were taken out of his hands when the event was cancelled because of labour troubles in France, and the two prototypes were sold off. Meanwhile Sutherland was also pursuing ways of reducing the production cost of the Mark II, and instigated a new engine design of two litres' capacity and with a single overhead camshaft. The patent Renwick &

Atom, seen here taking part in a rally in late 1945.

Bertelli valve and combustion chamber layout was retained, but inlet and exhaust manifolds changed sides since better results had been obtained with the spark plugs on the exhaust side. Bore and stroke were 78 x 102mm, giving a capacity of 1949cc. Various chassis changes were introduced at the same time, the most important being a move to hydraulic brakes.

A competition version was developed first, with dry-sump lubrication as hitherto, and this was offered to the public in the guise of a Speed Model, which was a replica of the works two-seaters, priced at a heady £875. In parallel, however, a cheaper model was introduced, to be known as the 15/98 and superseding the Mark II. The biggest difference was in the engine, which used wet-sump lubrication. By this time Harry Bertelli's workshop was involved in the production of the Graham British Special (later the Lammas-Graham), and he confined himself to producing special bodies. The standard offerings on the 15/98 chassis – a four-door saloon at £595, a two-door,

four-seater tourer at £575 and a drophead coupé – were produced by either Abbotts of Farnham or Abbey Coachworks of Acton, West London. There was also a 2/4-seater on the short chassis with bodywork by either Abbey Coachworks or Park Royal. Going to outside coachbuilders would have given Sutherland more opportunity to negotiate lower prices, but some believe that this also led to a drop in the quality of the bodywork.

The passing of the 1½-litre was mourned by some, and certainly in Mark II form it had been quite a commercial success with 166 examples sold. Sales understandably slackened during 1936 while the two new models were being introduced, and only a dozen or so Speed Models were sold during the year. However the 15/98 received a good press at that year's Motor Show, and with its 98bhp engine and 85mph top speed it was soon clear that it was going to be a worthy successor to the smaller car. The only sad note at the end of 1936 was that, possibly because of the company's withdrawal from competition, Bert Bertelli decided to move on. This left Gordon Sutherland in sole charge of the company, with Claude Hill as his right-hand man on the engineering side.

In 1938 sales started badly, and there was very little production. In order to clear stocks Sutherland reduced the prices of the 15/98 range substantially, the saloon and tourer now costing only £495. As for the Speed Model, he decided to take a pair of unsold chassis and clothe them with a radical new body. This had the then fashionable features associated with "streamlining": pontoon wings, cowled radiator, headlamps out of the slipstream and so on. Indeed to modern eyes it looks somewhat ahead of its time, more typical of the late 1940s than the 1930s, but this proved to be its undoing. The diehard traditionalists who were Aston Martin loyalists found the new car – dubbed the Type C – merely ugly, and sales struggled. Its price, at £775, was not in its favour, particularly as the very attractive Type 328 BMW was available at £695.

By the time that all production came to an end in 1940, some 144 15/98 models had been built. Of these about 15 were Speed Models, including the Type C. However, over the previous two years Sutherland and Hill had been engaged in some experimental work which was to have a profound effect on their future thinking, involving two prototype cars. The first had started life as a standard 15/98 saloon but had been fitted with a new all-steel four-door saloon body which used a steel box-section framework instead of the traditional ash. Many car manufacturers and coachbuilders were experimenting at this period with all-steel construction, all with the same intention of eliminating wood from the body framework. However

the Aston Martin approach was different to the extent that the box sections were rigid enough to add strength to the chassis – indeed, to become part of the whole car. Whether the two men intended this from the outset, or whether they only saw the system's possibilities when they started to consider the second prototype, is not clear.

The crudely-constructed framework, said to be ordinary electrical trunking, caused the car's roof height to be raised somewhat more than normal. Coupled with a shovel-shaped nose and a generally ungainly shape, this led to the car being affectionately known throughout the works as Donald Duck. Whatever the car's value in development terms, one can see in retrospect that its main achievement was to have prepared the ground for an even more influential prototype, known as Atom. This car was built during the summer of 1939, and could well have appeared at the 1939 Motor Show if such an event had taken place. It was again a four-door saloon, using the standard 15/98 engine, but everything else about it was unconventional. There was a chassis of sorts, but it merely formed part of what would now be called a spaceframe. This was built up in triangulated fashion, from square and rectangular section steel tubing, to form a combined chassis and body frame reaching up to the roof. Front suspension was independent, using the Gordon Armstrong cantilever system with coil springs and Armstrong piston-type shock absorbers. The engine was suspended from two mounting points to minimise vibration, and drove through a Cotal electrically-operated gearbox to a hypoid-bevel final drive.

On the framework was mounted a modern,

Atom's chassis was constructed from square and rectangular section steel tubing.

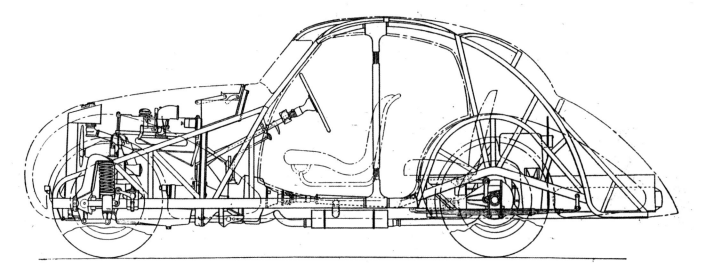

semi-streamlined body with concealed radiator, faired-in headlamps and a vee windscreen. However the body panels – steel rather than the preferred alloy, which had already become unobtainable – were neither stressed nor joined directly to the framework, but instead were formed over metal plates welded on at crucial points, with rubber inserts in between. Thus the system marked a fundamental divergence from what had been up to then the latest thinking on car design, which held that "integral construction" – where pressed-steel body panels provided the car's strength – was the way to go. As we now know, integral construction as practised just before WW2 – by, for example, Vauxhall and Citröen – was indeed widely adopted for volume production, but the tooling costs were prohibitive for smaller manufacturers. Sutherland and Hill were ahead of their time in developing an alternative, cost-effective system for the postwar Aston Martin.

Various commentators tried out the car in the

early years of the war, and were generally very impressed. Some were slightly disappointed that the attempt at streamlining had not gone far enough, since there were still separate wings instead of a full-width body. Others pointed out the fundamental drawback of an epicyclic gearbox, in that for reasons of sheer geometry close ratios are impossible. Nevertheless there was praise for the performance which the car managed to achieve on "Pool" petrol, and also for the steering and handling provided by the independent front suspension.

The company were fortunate in having at least one employee who was a conscientious objector and therefore could not be used on war work. Such development as could be carried out during the remainder of the war therefore fell to him. However, this was a very small proportion of the company's workload, the vast majority of which was given over throughout the period of hostilities to the Ministry of Aircraft Production.

Happily, Atom still exists and has been restored to a very high standard. Atom's original pre-war overhead camshaft engine has been replaced by one of the postwar pushrod design. Left: The selector for the Cotal epicyclic gearbox can be seen just below the central speedometer. Below: Atom's lines, with separate pontoon-style wings, betray the car's pre-war origins.

Chapter Two

David Brown Takes Over

Claude Hill (below left), the company's technical supremo throughout the wartime period, and David (later Sir David) Brown.

Although the name of David Brown is popularly associated with the early postwar history of the company, he did not enter the picture immediately. Initially Sutherland and Hill continued to develop both the Atom concept and a two-litre four-cylinder engine to propel it. Evidence of their commitment lay in their application as early as January 1945 – even before the war was won – to the Society of Motor Manufacturers and Traders to have the name Atom recorded against Aston Martin. In practice, of course, it was extremely difficult in those first postwar months to achieve very much in the way of actual production as both labour and materials, especially the latter, were in short supply. This probably explains the silence from the company, in terms of news, until the autumn of the following year.

Thus it was in October 1946 that the waiting enthusiasts learned that their beloved overhead-camshaft engine was to be no more, and that the new car was to have a completely new design of four-cylinder engine, using pushrods actuated by a chain-driven camshaft high in the block. The explanation given to the technical press was that this arrangement, coupled with the improved combustion-chamber space which it made possible, produced just as much power and yet allowed a "simpler" (and cheaper) design of cylinder head. Although the new engine had apparently performed well in bench testing it had clearly not yet been installed in a chassis. The only clues to the type of car in which it might appear were provided by The Motor, which stated that the construction would be of square-section tubes, as in the Atom, front suspension would be independent, and the body would be a four-door saloon; as things would turn out, the first two statements were true but the last certainly was not.

A few months later came the event which would mean that all such predictions were null and void. In February 1947 it was announced that Mr David Brown, of David Brown and Sons (Huddersfield) Ltd, "the well-known tractor and gear-cutting firm", had acquired the whole of the share capital of Aston Martin Ltd. David Brown were an old-established engineering firm with a very high reputation, who had started in the 19th century machining cast-iron gears for the textile mill trade and then been one of the first to change to steel. Their main factory was the Park Gear Works at Lockwood on the edge of Huddersfield, but they had other premises at Penistone to the south-east,

at Meltham Mills to the south, and at Farsley between Leeds and Bradford.

The David Brown in question, grandson of the founder, was born in 1904, and although apparently destined to inherit the business was certainly not offered an easy way into it. Instead he became an apprentice at the age of 17 and went through the normal pattern of training – fitting shop, foundry, pattern making, machine shop, drawing office, estimating and so on. While he was still an apprentice he was sent to South Africa in connection with a contract for installing gearboxes in gold mines, then back in England he helped with the development of centrifugal casting machines. Also – and surely unlike most apprentices – he spent time in America and on the Continent visiting various engineering factories. He presumably satisfied the family members about his ability, since at the tender age of 22 he found himself foreman of the worm gear department, and shortly afterwards was promoted to assistant works manager.

At about that time his father became ill and withdrew from the company, as a result of which he became a director of the company, aged 25. Two year later his uncle, who with David's father had been managing the business, died. David became joint managing director alongside a much older man, W S Roe. The tragic succession continued when within the year Roe died as well, and David Brown found himself sole managing director at the age of 28. Fortunately his ability shone through and the business prospered. His later business trips to America convinced him that there was a market opportunity for a British-made tractor, and he was responsible for the company branching out into the tractor business – firstly in conjunction with the inventor and tractor pioneer Harry Ferguson, and then, in 1939, in the form of a wholly-owned subsidiary, David Brown Tractors Ltd.

The first contact between Brown and Aston Martin had apparently come about through Brown answering an advertisement inserted by Gordon Sutherland anonymously in *The Times*. Sutherland, having struggled with the finances of the company ever since his family bought it, had decided to give up the struggle and sell out to a larger group which would have greater capital resources. Apparently Brown went as far as borrowing the Atom for an extended trial, as a result of which he formed a high opinion of its roadholding although a less favourable one of its power.

What was it about Aston Martin, however, that persuaded David Brown to buy the company? It was hardly the prospect of new business for his gear-cutting division, even though his firm had supplied worm-gear back axles some 17 years previously! Possibly it was that Brown saw a genuine opportunity to make money in the postwar car industry by buying up a known name and a prototype car for comparatively little money (£20,000). More likely, though, is that he was attracted by the glamour of association with a famous sporting car, and felt he could risk a certain amount of his own cash as long as he limited his exposure thereafter. Indeed at the time he acquired the company he confided to a contact that he had always wanted to build cars for the connoisseur.

Brown had been a sporting competitor himself in pre-war days in his Vauxhall Villiers supercharged special, winning numerous races at Southport Sands and achieving three class wins at the Shelsley Walsh hill-climb. How he acquired the car is an interesting story in itself. Apparently Amherst Villiers was experiencing problems with the gears of his superchargers and contacted the David Brown company. Brown junior was delegated to supervise the project, and this included being present when Villiers and his customer – the famous Raymond Mays – tested the installation on the car. At the young man's suggestion this was to take place early one morning on a highly suitable hill in the Pennines, not far from the factory.

Unfortunately Mays was late for the appointment, and rather than risk the traffic building up and spoiling the test Villiers suggested that Brown should drive the car. "I think he was surprised at the manner in which I conducted it up and down the hill", Brown reminisced, "which of course I knew backwards!" The outcome was that Villiers offered Brown a second car for a nominal price, provided he advertised the make of supercharger on the side of the bonnet.

An even deeper motivation for his interest in acquiring Aston Martin is suggested by John Wyer, who became Brown's Racing Manager in 1950. Wyer had hardly started his job before Brown told him that he wanted to be one of the Le Mans team drivers that year, driving a car of his own manufacture. This put Wyer in a difficult position; granted that Brown was by all accounts a highly skilled driver, he had neither the experience nor, probably, the stamina – he was in his mid-40s by then – for such a gruelling test. Wyer managed to avoid saying this to his boss's face by finding influential friends to say it for him, and embarrassment was avoided all round. Nevertheless the incident may

John Wyer, whom Brown brought in to the company initially as racing manager.

The 2.6-Litre Lagonda: its engine became the heart of the DB2 range.

be significant in revealing what might have been at the back of David Brown's mind when he bought the company.

Whatever Sutherland's motivation in selling, it was not to make a quick exit, as he agreed to stay on as a "technical director" (as did Claude Hill). The first priority, it was announced, would be to repair the Feltham works buildings, damaged by a flying bomb towards the end of the war, so that work could proceed on the new model. This decision was soon overtaken by events, however, when Brown decided that the original Victoria Road works were too small. He moved the main organisation to premises at nearby Hanworth Aero Park, leaving only the service department at Victoria Road. With all this disruption, just how much work was completed during 1947 is an open question. Certainly the company felt it necessary to indulge in some "teaser" public relations announcements, which the motoring press dutifully peddled in August and September of that year, implying that a full road test was only a matter of months away.

In any case David Brown was by no means able to devote his full attention to Aston Martin matters; as well as continuing to run his main business, he had also in September of that year acquired the Lagonda business from the serial entrepreneur Alan Good. The fact that the company was on the market had been vouchsafed to him by his local Lagonda distributor, Tony Scatchard, but Brown

was initially not interested. Yet when Lagonda was put into liquidation, the liquidator, J R Greenwood, whom Brown knew personally and who had also been made Lagonda's chairman, persuaded him to pay a visit to Staines to see what might be available.

The Lagonda assets included machinery and work-in-progress, an order book, some useful personnel and, importantly, a new W O Bentley-designed six-cylinder twin overhead camshaft engine of 2.6-litre capacity. Brown saw this engine, already tried and tested, as a long term solution for Aston Martin, and he was prepared to pay Greenwood what he thought was the reasonable sum of £50,000 for the business. However, three major manufacturers – Armstrong-Siddeley, Jaguar and Rootes – were also interested, and had been bidding sums in excess of £100,000. Brown expressed an interest at his own much lower figure and left, assuming that he was out of the reckoning. Some months later, though, everything had changed: a doubling of purchase tax on cars costing over £1000 had contributed to a general loss of optimism in the industry, and all three major bidders withdrew. Greenwood was sure that, apart from Brown, those who remained in contention had no thought of maintaining the business as a going concern, and therefore invited Brown back for a further discussion. He then conveniently left his office for a few minutes, leaving the bids in full view on his desk, and allowing Brown to work out that if he bid something over £50,000 then the Lagonda business was his.

Brown's winning bid was still a hefty (for those days) £52,500 for a package of assets which did not even include a building. An item in *The Times* said, "some time is likely to elapse before the machinery and stock are installed in new premises and production can be begun". It added that, "Mr Brown believes that the high quality British car has a big export future, and he says he has orders for the Lagonda amounting to nearly £500,000 from the United States alone". How many of those orders could still be counted on, however, when the previous owners had already announced the cancellation of their plans for Lagonda production, is a matter of conjecture. The company line about export potential was repeated in the motoring press, and *The Autocar* hinted at what was behind it: Brown needed a steel allocation, for which export production received priority in those days of postwar restrictions. In the end Brown had to prime the pump at Feltham with the loan of some steel from his main business.

Since the Staines premises had to be vacated, Brown leased some hangars close to the Aston Martin building on the Hanworth Aero Park, and Lagonda moved in during January and February 1948. Together the two companies formed what was to be known as the Aston-Martin-Lagonda division of David Brown Ltd, and the process of integrating the two organisations began. Clearly Brown had had no intention of replicating Lagonda's manufacturing facilities at Feltham when he already had a world-class set-up in the North of England. Accordingly manufacture of engines, chassis and gearboxes moved up to his factory at Farsley, near Leeds, although engine work later moved to the Meltham (Huddersfield) factory. This left design, bodywork and assembly at Feltham, together with the service department and an embryonic racing section. The personnel also began to come together, and before long there was a common General Manager for the two marques in the shape of James Stirling. He was an appointment from within David Brown Tractors, and thus owed allegiance to neither side. However he had had previous automotive experience with the Vauxhall company. The Chief Draughtsman, on the other hand – Frank Ayto – had come from Lagonda, and before that had been with the Bentley company at Cricklewood. Nevertheless there was initially very much a "them and us" spirit within the two groups of employees, not helped by the split site with some of the older Aston Martin hands still located at Victoria Road.

Possibly the most influential of all the ex-Lagonda personnel was Frank Feeley, the highly regarded body designer, who had made his reputation before the war with a series of dramatic body styles on such cars as the LG6 and the V-12. Feeley had in fact been sacked from Lagonda when the old company decided to cancel production plans for the postwar car, and was out of work for several months until Brown made contact with him and invited him to work at the new company. He of course accepted, but he found it difficult to see very much work coming his way in the short term, and so things turned out. Looking back on that period, he described the scene in bleak terms. "That first winter of 1947-48 was quite traumatic for me really in so much as I arrived at Feltham to find these big aircraft hangars there and dumped in the middle of them were piles of materials, some jigs for the V12 car – not many – and various bits and pieces that came as a result of the acquisition of the Lagonda name.

That's all we had! I used to get very depressed; I did a bit of work on the forerunner of the new Lagonda but nothing really very much."

In fact those early months proved so frustrating that he decided to join the coachbuilding firm Jack Barclay, but when he put in his notice Brown would not hear of it and persuaded Feeley to stay on. "During that time we had power cuts frequently, awful winter months and desperate shortages of steel. It was a very difficult time and although I stayed on I did nothing very much, merely doodling around putting various ideas down on paper on the new Lagonda." To keep him occupied, Brown sent him to Italy to find design ideas – a trip which was to bear fruit in the 1949 Le Mans cars and their successor, the DB2.

Thereafter Feeley was very much a one-man band on the bodybuilding side. He described his relationship with Brown in some detail. "Perhaps I took the lead more than I would normally have done, but it seemed to me that David Brown, having bought Lagonda and Aston Martin, then did not know quite what to do with them. He'd got the companies and he'd been used to driving motor cars of quality but not making them. He was an engineer all the same and had an engineering business but of quite a different sort, and maybe you can persuade yourself that you know all there is to know on the subject. He didn't really but he certainly had great enthusiasm and drive." In another comment on the man, he added, "unlike the endless arguments we had at Staines, with David Brown we got an immediate decision".

Although Feeley was underemployed others certainly were not. The two-litre pushrod engine which was to power the new car had already been announced, but the chassis into which it was to be installed had not. This was the subject of increasingly frenzied activity during that winter of 1947-48, and the results would not be long in appearing.

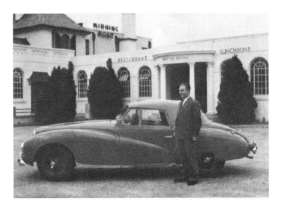

Frank Feeley, seen with a Two-Litre Sports drophead coupe.

Chapter Three

The Two-Litre Sports (DB1)

Section through the four-cylinder pushrod engine of the Two-Litre Sports.

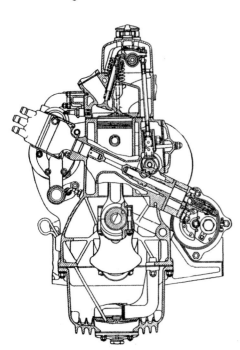

At last, in the spring of 1948, Aston Martin enthusiasts were given something more substantial on which they could feast. This was first a full description, and then driving impressions, of the car which was officially named the Two-Litre Sports (but which eventually came to be known, retrospectively, as the DB1). They had been told, some 18 months earlier, that it was to be a four-cylinder pushrod design, but now came further details of the engine and of the chassis in which it was to be mounted.

The pushrod valve actuation permits a combustion chamber layout whereby the inlet valve is set vertically over the piston while the exhaust valve is inclined over a pocket at the offside. This allows a smooth exit passage for the exhaust gases, although it requires a somewhat unusual manifold arrangement arching away from the side of the head. The head is unusual in other ways as well, such as having horizontal plugs sited alarmingly close to the head/block face. As we have seen, the apparently retrograde move from the traditional overhead camshaft to pushrod actua-

tion was justified by the company at the time as simplifying the head design without any loss in power. In a later interview Claude Hill amplified his thinking on this subject. "I sought simplicity ... I could get the same power more quietly and more smoothly from my new pushrod engine with its special valve positioning as we got from the ohc 2-litre. Moreover it is easier to manufacture, is easier to maintain and by eliminating dry-sump lubrication saves the cost of one oil-pump and obviates long warming-up periods, oil-joints that might leak and a vulnerable oil-tank."

Elsewhere there is evidence that the design was aimed at robustness and long life, the crankshaft having five main bearings and notably large-diameter main- and big-end bearings; their diameters are 2.48in and 2in respectively, and the bearing surfaces are formed from white-metal strip. Further evidence of the desire to reduce stress on the crankshaft can be found in the location of the timing chain, which – most unusually – is situated at the rear of the engine. This practice, to be found in very few cars at the time (Alvis is the example which springs to mind) is presumably intended to minimise torsional vibrations. The duplex chain also drives the water pump, and a skew gear from the camshaft drives a diagonal shaft which takes the drive to the distributor at its upper end and the oil pump at the other. Oil circulation, via a full-flow filter, is mainly via drilled passageways rather than pipework, and the camshaft bearings sit in their own oil bath. Coolant output from the pump is directed at the cylinder head, and particularly at

the area around the plugs, while cooling of the block relies on thermosyphon action. At the front of the engine is a conventional belt drive for the fan and dynamo, the fan running on a substantial shaft which also forms the front engine mounting.

Block and crankcase are a single iron casting, and both sump and rocker cover are in light alloy, with ribbed reinforcement. Although the capacity of the new engine is almost identical to its predecessor at 1970cc in place of 1950cc, its bore and stroke at 82.5mm x 92mm respectively are radically different. These dimensions were no doubt adopted in anticipation of the new taxation formula which no longer penalised an engine's bore size; the new engine approaches "square" dimensions, with a stroke to bore ratio of 1.12:1, as against 1.31:1 for its predecessor. The pistons each have three compression rings and one scraper, and the gudgeon pins are fully floating. Both pistons and connecting rods are of light alloy. Carburation is via twin SUs, with an auxiliary solenoid-operated carburettor for starting.

A Borg and Beck clutch connects the drive to a four-speed gearbox of David Brown design which is in unit with the engine and has synchromesh on the upper three gears. This layout differs both from earlier company statements, which talked of a separate gearbox, and from Atom which used a Cotal electrically-operated box. The engine/gearbox assembly sits on flexible mountings front and rear. The front one is formed from the fan-spindle shaft, set in rubber, while the rear one is adjacent to the flywheel and also sits on

rubber. The drive is via a divided propeller shaft with a rubber-mounted centre bearing, to a 4.1:1 hypoid-bevel rear axle.

This engine/transmission combination is mounted in a chassis which is immediately recognisable as being derived from that of Atom. Formed as before from a mixture of square- and rectangular-section tubes welded together, it differs from Atom in one main respect: since the chassis is intended to support both closed and open bodywork, it can no longer rely on the inherent strength of the roof framework which Atom used. The strength has therefore had to be added to the mid-

Frank Feeley's design was as up-to-date as any British car at the time.

This shot clearly shows the unusual exhaust manifold arrangement, arching upwards to meet the exhaust pipe

DB1 chassis. Note the parallel horizontal side tubes and the trailing arm front suspension.

RICHE.

portion of the chassis, in the form of doubled-up side members. These parallel tubes, three inches deep and of 13-gauge steel, are welded together via spacers at intervals and in effect form substantial box members at the heart of the chassis. They are separated by channel section crossmembers underneath, and by a latticework superstructure of 18-gauge rectangular tubes front and back which form respectively the engine compartment plus bulkhead and the tail compartment for luggage and the petrol tank. Joints are gas- or arc-welded according to their position. Claude Hill recounted that he chose rectangular tubing rather than round section as it was so much easier to handle, and in particular to weld together, since different sizes can be made to mate up along a common joint face by skilful choice of the mitre angle. A further advantage is that the flat surfaces which rectangular tubing offers make attaching other components a much simpler job.

It is worth noting at this point some comments, much later, from body designer Frank Feeley. According to his account the decision to use an open rather than closed body was a very late one, taken by Brown against the advice of Claude Hill. The doubled-up side members were thus a last-minute attempt to strengthen a chassis which up to that point had been very similar to the Atom

design. Even so the strengthening was, in Feeley's view, insufficient; he went so far as to say that he "never saw such a weak car". Certainly the additional side members, being in the same horizontal plane as the original ones, would have added relatively little beam strength in this crucial area, and in practice there were problems of door fit when the chassis was loaded up. It could well be that this tendency never showed itself during the development of the prototype, which had virtually no bodywork until a short time before its first race.

The front suspension again is recognisably similar to Atom's, in that it is independent and employs coil springs. The main difference is that it is now of double trailing arm design; the upper arm is still formed by the Armstrong piston-type damper, but this component is now mounted in front of the axle line instead of behind. The lower arm is a substantial component pivoting on a combination of needle-roller and ball bearings. Another difference is that instead of the anti-roll bar being a conventional external fitting, it is now a simple straight bar which is splined into the two suspension arm pivots and therefore concealed within the front cast aluminium crossmember. This tubular member is filled with oil and thus provides permanent lubrication for the trailing-arm bearings. The coil springs themselves are of 4½in diameter

and made from 15/32in gauge stock. A Marles steering box is linked to a central bellcrank lever which in turn actuates separate trackrods; the bellcrank pivot is on needle-roller bearings which are permanently lubricated from the oil-filled front crossmember.

At the rear the suspension for the live axle differs from Atom in that it also uses coil springs, whereas Atom had conventional leaf springs. This permitted Hill to use semi-trailing arms to locate the axle, their rearward ends being attached close to the outer ends of the axle and the forward ends pivoting from brackets nearer to the centre-line of the car, mounted on a very substantial crossmember. Hill much preferred this arrangement to leaf springs for several reasons, the main one being that it was more effective in countering brake torque reaction. In addition there is an "antisway" (Panhard) rod linking one end of the axle with the chassis on the opposite side; Armstrong dampers are again employed. The coil springs are of the same diameter as at the front but of ½in gauge, giving a frequency of 100 cycles per minute compared with 90 at the front. Braking is via a Girling hydraulic system, using 12in cast-iron drums with two leading shoes at the front. The drums are set almost totally within the width of the 5.75 x 16in knock-off type wire wheels.

This is chassis AMC/49/6, originally built as a three-seater roadster and later converted to a drophead coupe.

The "49" in the chassis number indicates the year of manufacture.

The overall effect of this design was to provide a frame which was substantially stiffer than that of any previous Aston Martin, which then permitted the adoption of much "softer" (low periodicity) suspension than was the norm at the time. In this respect it marked a significant move forward from the "vintage" school of design, which had combined a relatively whippy chassis with stiffer suspension. Hill's objectives had been to provide "a simple construction that would lend itself to comparatively small-scale production, first-class steering and roadholding, and a car capable of a genuine 90mph and really comfortable riding". To achieve this he felt it "essential to employ really soft springs to obtain truly comfortable riding, and I was confident that I could do this without

The rear window has no doubt been substantially enlarged compared with the original design.

destroying sports-car controllability".

One aspect of the car where *The Autocar* article was unable to give any detailed description was the matter of bodywork. All it could say was that a modern, streamlined form of four-seater body would be standardised. This rather contradicted a report in the issue of *The Motor* only two days previously, which stated confidently that the new car would be an "open sports 2-4-seater". Anyone studying the drawing of the chassis frame would have wondered how two rows of seats could possibly be fitted in, and they would have continued to wonder when reading the driving impressions of the same magazine's joint Technical Editor, Joseph Lowrey, a couple of months later. The ballasted prototype which he drove had virtually no bodywork at all, but the two seats which were installed appeared to take up all the available room. Lowrey was clearly impressed, commenting on the fact that "suspension which gives a boulevard ride at low speeds gives no trace of float at high speeds ... the car adheres quietly and evenly to the road however hard it is accelerated, braked or cornered". Interestingly, he comments that "there is provision for the fitting of an anti-roll bar, but this

does not seem to be needed on the open car".

Accompanying Lowrey during this test drive had been St John ("Jock") Horsfall, whose official title was Assistant to the Technical Director, Claude Hill. In practice Horsfall was employed purely for his skills as a test driver, refining the design and testing modifications as they were installed on the car. His qualifications for the job included much competition experience in an Aston Martin of his own, a Two-Litre Speed Model, in which he had scored numerous successes in 1938, including a class win in the Donington TT, and with which he had won the 1946 Belgian Grand Prix outright. He had also acquired a formidable reputation during the war as a high-speed courier working for MI6. David Brown, as someone who had himself competed with an Aston Martin in pre-war days, knew Horsfall and had brought him into the company. Horsfall had been fully employed ever since in developing the new Two-Litre model, which involved driving it, in his own words, "flat out, this being 90mph or over for miles and miles on end. I would do this in the early hours of the morning and used to reckon on covering 150 to 200 miles every night – and it was cold!"

Horsfall was now to come into the picture even more prominently. It began with Hill and himself allowing two outside experts to try the car – Fred Dixon and Tony Rolt. Dixon, in particular, was highly experienced as both a development mechanic and a driver, and he was so impressed that he asked Jock when the company was going to race it. This was enough for Hill and Horsfall to take the idea seriously, and they decided to approach David Brown with a proposal that the car should be entered for that year's Spa 24-hour race in July – the premier sports-car race of the year, since Le Mans had not yet been revived. With Brown's known long-term intention of entering the competition world, there was only one likely outcome, and the pair received the necessary permission. However that was the easy part; the race was only nine weeks away, and Hill decided to fit a special two-seater body, which would require the design and manufacture of a modified frame, partly to permit a larger fuel tank. To add to the pressure, the management then decided that the first prototype car had to be made ready as well, to act as a reconnaissance and back-up car, and this meant designing and making yet another body from scratch.

Since this is a fairy story, and all fairy stories have a happy ending, it should be recorded here and now that the team succeeded in building the new car, preparing the second, and arriving with them both at Spa on time. This simple statement should not, however, be allowed to conceal the magnificent achievement which lies behind it: Hill, Horsfall and the team behind them worked literally night and day for weeks on end. The new body, it was decided, should for reasons of minimal air resistance be no wider than the chassis, which implied separate wings rather in the style of the last pre-war cars. Furthermore the Spa circuit demanded high gearing, yet the highest hypoid ratio available was a mere 3.9:1. The answer was to increase the rear wheel size from 16in to 19in (the fronts were 18in, just to confuse matters), reinforcing the impression that this was in fact a pre-war car. Nevertheless the effect on the aerodynamics was impressive, testified to by a 110mph maximum and an average fuel consumption during the race of 22mpg.

There are legendary tales of the attention to detail which went into preparing the race car. Horsfall added many touches based on his racing experience: auxiliary gravity tanks for both fuel and oil, a wiper for the aero screen (which proved

more than useful during the race) and extra padding round the cockpit. Fortunately Horsfall and his co-driver, Leslie Johnson, were of much the same build, so there was no need to make adjustments each time there was a change of driver. Engine modifications were confined to stronger valve springs and an increase in compression ratio from the standard 7.3:1 to 8.5:1. In the meantime a miraculous effort on the second car had resulted in it bearing an attractive drophead coupé body, finished in light blue.

Even so not every job had been completed when the two cars left the factory for the Dover ferry to Belgium – in fact every mechanic working on either of the two cars had to write down exactly which of his jobs he had not been able to finish so that work could be resumed when the team arrived at Spa. Moreover there had been no time for any serious testing, which meant that the allotted time for practice had to be used for this purpose. It brought to light another problem: the clutch needed adjusting, but the only way to reach it was by cutting a hole in the undershield, and so more valuable time was wasted. In the end Horsfall had time for a few exploratory laps in the back-up "Blue" car – essential, since unlike Johnson he had never raced at the circuit. Typically, he nevertheless managed to put up the fastest practice lap in any class, at night in the pouring rain. As for the race car itself, there was just time on the day before the race to take it out for a few exploratory laps to check that everything was working.

Horsfall and Johnson's special-bodied Two-Litre on the way to winning the 1948 Spa 24-Hour race.

The "Blue" car – the prototype drophead, which acted as back-up car for the Spa race.

There is room for a passenger in the rear, at a squeeze.

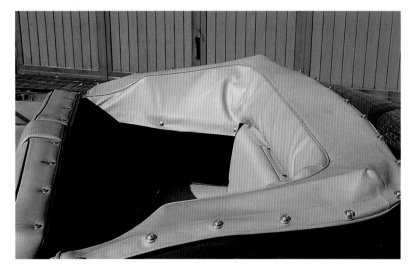

The race ran, like Le Mans, from 4.00pm on the Saturday to 4.00pm on the Sunday. As well as the new Horsfall/Johnson car there were three other Aston Martins in the race, all (of course) pre-war cars. For the watching Aston Martin personnel things could hardly have begun in a worse fashion as after only one lap Horsfall came into the pits. It would hardly have been a surprise if the new car, not even properly tested, had retired there and then, but the truth was much less serious. Horsfall had been understandably worried when he saw that both the water temperature and the oil pres-

sure gauges were reading too high. It transpired that the temperature gauge was faulty and that the oil pressure was higher than in practice because the oil had been changed for one of a heavier grade. From then on the two drivers reeled in the laps faultlessly, relying on a pre-arranged plan which ensured that they did not exceed 4300rpm in any gear, equivalent to about 100mph in top, which according to Horsfall required no more than half throttle to maintain.

Before the race, the V12 Ferrari to be driven by Chinetti had seemed to offer the greatest threat to the new Aston Martin in its class (1500-2000cc), but in the event it only lasted four hours, retiring with a blown gasket. Other strong competitors in the class were the Gerard/Louveau Delage, the Scaron/Veyron Simca, Wisdom's Healey saloon and the Alta driven by George Abecassis. In the race as a whole there were further formidable entries, including such names as Delahaye and Talbot. The weather conditions were atrocious, heavy rain making the road surface slippery for all but the last hour and occasional mist further adding to the drivers' difficulties. There were numerous retirements through cars leaving the circuit, and others for mechanical reasons, but Horsfall and Johnson continued their steady progress through the field. They had led their class ever since the Abecassis Alta left the road during the night, but it was soon

The drophead coupé is just as elegant with its hood up.

apparent that their average speed was better than anything else on the circuit – attributable partly, no doubt, to the conditions, but also to a great degree to the new Aston Martin's phenomenal road-holding.

And so it came to pass that the new, untested, untried Two-Litre Aston Martin not only survived the whole 24 hours, not only won its class in this great race, but trounced cars of more than twice its engine size to win the race outright at an average speed of 71.84mph. Interestingly, Horsfall, the newcomer to the circuit, put up a fastest lap of 6min 52sec, whereas Johnson's fastest was 6min 55 sec. Out of 40 starters only 23 finished. After the race Horsfall even drove the winning car home, and he greatly enjoyed the drive. The whole story is indeed a fairy tale, and a more sensational manner of launching a new model could hardly be imagined. Perhaps the only disappointment is that the car's appearance did it less than justice, especially compared with the beautiful lines of the "Blue" car which accompanied it to Spa. Sammy Davis, Sports Editor of *The Autocar*, could perhaps be excused when he referred to the winning car in his race report as "the 1938 Aston", as it certainly looked like a car from that era.

The "Blue" car (chassis AMC/48/2, reg THX 231) was the prototype of the mere 14 examples of the Two-Litre Sports which eventually reached the public. The company made a parallel attempt to sell the alternative open sports body style as a "Spa Replica". The rebuilt Spa car (originally given the chassis number SPA/48/1, later changed to LMA/48/1 – reg THX 259) appeared under this guise (to get round the rule banning competition cars!) at the 1948 Earls Court Show, Britain's first postwar Show. Alongside it was an example of the drophead coupé – AMC/48/7, TME 474. It soon became clear, however, that there was insufficient interest to make a production run of the open sports style worthwhile, and the project was

Indicators are concealed in the front wings.

Frank Feeley designed the central portion of the radiator grille to echo the pre-war radiator shape.

Compartments in the front wings are for tools and the spare wheel; Feeley continued a pre-war Lagonda practice.

dropped. No doubt the asking price was a factor in putting off buyers, since at £3109 it would have cost one-third more than the drophead coupé. By contrast the drophead version was well received when it was officially launched just before the Show. It was only at this point that the company dropped any pretence of the car being a four-seater, or even a "2-4-seater", revealing that it had just a single bench seat which would accommodate the driver plus two passengers. Even so, they clung to the possibility of squeezing in a fourth person; the description in *The Motor* (which reads as if it was copied straight from the company's press release) states that behind the bench seat "there is a large luggage compartment which can form additional under-the-hood seating accommodation".

The lines of the drophead coupé –another Frank Feeley design – are advanced for the period, and stand comparison with those of the iconic Jaguar XK120 which was launched at the same time. The convex curve of the separate front wing blends gracefully into the door area, creating a virtually full-width body, while the rear wings, also semi-separate, bear traces of Feeley's pre-war art deco influences in having curved spats over the wheel arches. The radiator grille is of a shape reminiscent of the pre-war cars, and is flanked by two smaller grilles which admit air for cooling the front brakes. The actual construction of the body was also advanced; although there is a normal opening panel in the bonnet, the bonnet and front wings are manufactured in one piece so that the whole assembly can be removed easily for access to the engine and front suspension. Concealed within the offside front wing is the spare wheel, another throwback to Feeley's Lagonda days, and there are twin fuel fillers in the rear wings. The windscreen is of vee design, with two flat panes – a compromise arrived at because it was impossible to obtain curved glass at that period, and one-piece flat screens were judged to look too "pre-war".

Inside, the one-piece bench seat is so wide that

The Feeley-designed instrument panel bears no resemblance to the pre-war Aston Martin layout.

it was initially difficult for the driver to adjust it unaided, and it had to have a special spring-loaded mechanism designed to make both ends move in parallel. Feeley laid out the instrument panel from scratch, with no reference to pre-war Aston Martin practice. It has the tachometer and speedometer directly in front of the driver, with the ignition switch on his right and smaller dials to the left. There is a single large glovebox at the far left-hand side. The chassis itself is unchanged, using the standard 4.1:1 final drive with 16in wheels. The engine, with the normal 7.25:1 compression ratio, was quoted as producing 90bhp. A high compression "Spa" head was offered as an extra, which raised the output to 95bhp.

The drophead was priced at £1498 basic plus £833 purchase tax, giving a total of £2331. This placed it firmly in the ranks of the more exclusive cars on the market – cheaper than the Bristol or Healey saloons, on a par with the Healey roadster, but more expensive, by some distance, than any of the Allards or the new Jaguar XK120. High import duties ruled out any non-British alternatives from meaningful comparison. Given that the new Morris Minor cost £358 and the Austin A40 saloon £463, there would have been relatively few buyers able

to contemplate the showroom price of the Aston Martin. This, together with the fact that there was no saloon or fixed-head coupé style on offer, and that it was a four-cylinder competing with sixes or even V8s, must go some way towards accounting for the tiny sales of the Two-Litre.

There must also be a suspicion that David Brown's heart was not in this particular project, and that other happenings at Feltham were demanding his attention. For a start, three key people – Sutherland, Hill and Horsfall – left the company in the first half of 1949. In Sutherland's case it was to give his full time to running his other interest, the Abbott coachbuilding business in Farnham, Surrey. By staying on with Aston Martin for a couple of years he had at least ensured continuity. Horsfall decided to concentrate on his career as a racing driver, having completed the chassis testing for which he had been recruited, but sadly he was killed in the August of that year while racing an ERA at Silverstone. There is also the possibility that Horsfall was influenced by Hill, with whom he was particularly friendly.

Claude Hill's departure was after more than 20 years of (almost) continuous employment with the company. It is said that the break came about as a

The handbrake is placed on the driver's right, to allow three-abreast seating if necessary.

The interior trim is of high quality without being luxurious.

result of a disagreement over the matter of a six-cylinder engine. Hill had been working on a six-cylinder version of his pushrod engine for the previous three years, and it was clearly his intention to install it in the Two-Litre chassis. Yet when David Brown became involved he suggested, with some logic, that he would rather use the engine which already existed within the Group, namely the Lagonda engine, which had the additional merit (in the eyes of many, but perhaps not Claude Hill) of having twin overhead camshafts. Hill was right in that his design would probably have produced as much power as any dohc engine, but Brown was probably right to give himself a "high-tech" story to tell his American customers in the

face of Ferrari's V12 wizardry. There is general agreement that this was the prime cause for Hill leaving the company, with Brown insisting on using the Lagonda engine while Hill fought a rear-guard action for his own design. Something must have been in the wind when Bill Boddy of *Motor Sport* spoke to Hill in March 1949 about the Spa car, since he finished with the prescient comment, "it is to be hoped that Claude Hill will not relinquish development of his most intriguing motor car". Hill soon took up the position of Chief Engineer with Ferguson Research, later FF Developments, working on four wheel drive systems, and remained there up to his retirement in 1971.

In addition to managing his way through these personnel changes, Brown was pursuing a works team entry in the newly revived Le Mans race. This involved major changes to both chassis and bodywork, and in one case to the engine as well. The main work on the chassis followed a decision, based on advice from Horsfall, to shorten the wheelbase by no less than nine inches, bringing the dimension down to 8ft 3in. This had been the intention with the Spa car the previous year, but there had been no time to implement it. As to the body, Brown (one assumes it was he) took the fundamental decision to move away from open bodywork and instead use the more aerodynamic lines of a closed coupé. Again Frank Feeley was responsible for the design, which shows the influence of his trip round the Italian coachbuilding industry referred to in the previous chapter. The resulting shape has clear overtones of Italian styling at the time, with the flowing wing lines of a semi-full width body brilliantly blending into a "fastback" tail. Looking at the finished result, if one had to guess where Feeley had spent most time in Italy one might say that it was at Pinin Farina.

The body in fact bore all the hallmarks of the subsequent DB2, and in that respect can be regarded as the forerunner of that model. As on the production Two-Litre model, the bonnet and front wings were made as one unit, but unlike that model – and presaging the DB2 – there was no separately-opening bonnet panel. Instead the whole bonnet/wing unit was hinged at the front and could be opened forwards, giving virtually unobstructed access to both engine and front suspension. The three-piece grille of the Two-Litre was retained but lower and wider, with wider spacing to the vertical bars. Needless to say the Le Mans cars were two-seaters, and the majority of the

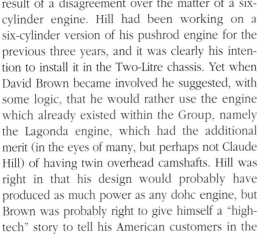

The pivoting screen and fixed quarter-light form a complex construction.

The windscreen folds flat on to the bonnet.

Right: The GB plate is proof that the car is used for serious motoring.

Aston Martin made their own bodies for the small numbers of Two-Litre Sports produced.

W O Bentley was Chief Engineer of the Lagonda company during the time it was being developed, its detailed design was completed around 1943 by Willie Watson, who had been with Lagonda since the 1930s. (Watson was to reappear at Feltham in 1952.) Of 2.6-litre capacity, the engine's most interesting feature from a performance point of view was its twin overhead camshaft valve arrangement. This was almost unique on a British car at the time, the only other such engine being that of the short-lived Invicta Black Prince, which was another Willie Watson design. Other points were hemispherical combustion chambers, detachable wet liners and a "barrel" type crankcase in which the crankshaft complete with its main bearings and their housings was inserted from one end. It was already in production at David Brown's Leeds factory and being installed in the Lagonda saloon.

The highly experienced John Eason Gibson was appointed team manager for the 1949 Le Mans project and he supervised the cars' preparation. This included once again the use of 18in wheels, giving a rather ungainly stance to what was otherwise an attractive streamlined design. The drivers were Leslie Johnson and Charles Brackenbury in the prototype car, with Arthur Jones/Nick Haines and Pierre Maréchal/"Taso" Mathieson in the two-litre cars. The race itself began badly for the team, with Leslie Johnson bringing the six-cylinder car into the pits after only six laps. The problem was apparently simple and easy to fix; an air-lock in the cooling system had forced all the coolant out of the system. Unfortunately refilling it entailed breaking the seals before the necessary laps had

space behind the seats was taken up by a large fuel tank. A three-car team was built for the race, two of them – chassis LMA/49/1 (reg UMC 64) and LMA/49/2 (UMC 65) – having the four-cylinder engine, and the third – LML/49/3 (UMC 66) – having the six-cylinder Lagonda engine installed (note the change in chassis code-letter to denote a different type of engine). The third car was entered under the new Le Mans "Prototype" regulations, which avoided the homologation requirement to show that a production run was under way. This was presumably the source of the disagreement between Hill and Brown, with Hill wanting time to develop his six-cylinder design and Brown needing something more urgently.

It was now up to Brown to demonstrate that the Lagonda engine was capable of standing up to the demands of a 24-hour race. To Brown it would have looked a gamble worth taking. He could see that to compete effectively in his chosen price bracket he badly needed a six-cylinder engine, and that this was particularly true in the US market where he was planning to make most of his sales. Commonly known as a "Bentley" engine, because

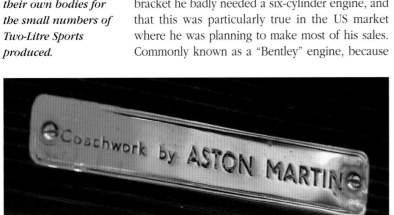

been completed, which meant compulsory retirement. Later inspection, however, revealed a fundamental design fault in the layout of the cooling system, which would have led to the coolant loss recurring and to inevitable retirement.

The two remaining Aston Martins circulated steadily throughout the evening and night, with Maréchal and Mathieson in particular working their way steadily up the leader board. By midnight they were eighth, and by early morning fifth, with the second car eleventh after a long pit stop. However Maréchal had complained about lack of brakes, and at about midday disaster struck: the car overturned and poor Maréchal was taken to hospital, where he later died. It transpired that the car had been losing hydraulic fluid. Jones and Haines went on to take seventh place, a small comfort for an otherwise sad and disappointing weekend.

Three weeks later, however, at the Spa 24-hour race, the cars more than made up for their Le Mans showing. Johnson and Brackenbury again drove the 2.6-litre prototype UMC 66, and brought it in third (and second in its class) behind a Ferrari and a Delage. These last two provided high drama towards the end of the race; the Delage began to lose oil and power, and the Ferrari spun on the oil. Both managed to stagger to the finish, and only just kept ahead of the Aston Martin. Nick Haines, accompanied this time by Lance Macklin, took a two-litre car (UMC 65) to fifth place and third in its class. These results were highly encouraging; the move to six cylinders seemed to have been vindicated, and apart from weak shock absorbers the cars seem to have shown up no major problems during the race.

In what was becoming a rather protracted development programme, the factory had constructed a second six-cylinder prototype, chassis LML/49/4 (UMC 272). This was much closer to a normal production car, since unlike the racing versions it was fully trimmed, and its wheels had reverted to the normal 16in size, greatly improving its appearance. Four large louvres had been added on each side of the bonnet behind the wheel arches in an attempt to improve brake cooling, and the rear portion instead of containing a long-range fuel tank was fitted up as a luggage compartment. Built in July 1949, it had been driven by Brown himself the following month to the International Trophy meeting at Silverstone, where Lance Macklin was allowed to demonstrate it round the circuit. (Incidentally Macklin later bought it outright in order to enter the 1950 Targa Florio. He replaced the SU

Coats by Joy Ricardo Ltd. of London.

carburettors with triple Webers and did well in the race until he crashed, doing so much damage that he had to sell the car to pay for the repairs.)

However it was not until January 1950 – some six months after the Spa race – that the motoring public was allowed to read anything substantial about the impending new model. This was when the car featured in an article by Laurence Pomeroy, the other joint Technical Editor of *The Motor*, when he accompanied James Watt, the newly-appointed head of the Automobile Division of David Brown Ltd, on a Continental tour. Pomeroy clearly jumped at the opportunity, as he knew the qualities of both the Lagonda engine and the Two-Litre chassis, describing the latter as one "which had already

Aston Martin advertising in 1949 majored on their sporting heritage (note the vignette of Horsfall's Spa car)

Start of the 1949 Le Mans, with one of the DB1 saloons disappearing fast out of the picture.

aroused the enthusiasm of the critics by reason of its unusually good suspension and road-holding characteristics". The two men covered nearly 1000 miles in four days, embracing Paris, Le Mans and Brussels.

On these Routes Nationales Pomeroy found it easy to average 60mph over long distances, thanks to road-holding and steering which he described as "truly superb". He was equally impressed with the car's "astonishing" performance, managing more than once to reach a speed of 105mph. "It is important to emphasise that these outstanding figures were obtained on a car which was taken straightaway from everyday use on the road, and tuned so as to give such flexibility on top gear that one had no occasion to depart from this ratio unless the speed fell below 10mph". The car's fuel consumption varied between 19 and 23mpg – "highly creditable at the speeds realised". Pomeroy's only real complaint concerned the shock absorbers, which, he implied, had virtually ceased to work by the second half of the trip. "I

shall be surprised," he added, "if the equipment on the production cars is not considerably different from the somewhat puny device upon which we were relying." He also made clear his dislike of the steering column gearchange, and mentioned in passing the "prominent" exhaust note, a point which others would refer to in later years.

Overall it was clear that Pomeroy, who was a very experienced engineer, tester and journalist, was impressed. "One feels that the 2½-litre six-cylinder Aston Martin will prove an immense attraction to those discerning drivers who seek performance of very high order with smooth running and delicacy of control." Throughout his article Pomeroy described the car as the "Le Mans type 2½-litre six-cylinder Aston Martin". He recognised that for obvious reasons it could no longer bear the Two-Litre name, yet it also seems clear that the company had not yet chosen a new one for the model which was about to enter production. That would have to await its official unveiling some two months later.

DB1 – Summary Statistics

Engine

configuration	4 cylinders in line, overhead valves, pushrods
capacity	1970cc
bore	82.55mm
stroke	92mm
RAC rating	16.9hp
compression ratio	7.25:1
firing order	1342
valve timing	inlet opens 10° atdc,
tappet clearances (cold)	.012in
brake horsepower	90 @ 4750rpm
crankshaft	
no of bearings	5
main bearing	2.48in (63mm) diameter
big end	2in (51mm) diameter
crankcase capacity	1½ gallons (6.8 litres)
cooling system	pump for head, thermo-syphon for cylinders, capacity 3¼ galls (14.8 litres)
ignition details	coil, 12 volts
contact breaker gap	.012-.015in
plugs – make/gap	Lodge HNP 14mm/.022in
carburettors	Twin SU horizontal
fuel pump	Twin SU electric
clutch	Borg & Beck single plate

Gearbox

type	David Brown 4-speed
gear ratios	4.1, 5.17, 7.7 and 12.0 to 1; reverse 12.0:1

Chassis

wheelbase	108in (2743mm)
track	54in (1372mm)
length	176in (4470mm)
width	65½in (1664mm)
weight (dry)	2520lb (1143kg)
turning circle	35ft (10.7m)
suspension	independent at front, live axle at rear, coil springs all round
wheels and tyres	Dunlop centre-lock wires, 5.75 x 16in
tyre pressures	27psi all round
brakes	Girling hydraulic (2LS at front), drums 12in diameter
steering box	Marles worm and roller
propeller shaft	Hardy Spicer, divided
rear axle	hypoid bevel
ratio	4.1:1
shock absorbers	Armstrong piston-type hydraulic
petrol tank capacity	14½ galls (66 litres)

Prices (excl. purchase tax)

drophead coupé	1948: £1498
open sports	1948: £1998

Numbers produced

drophead coupé	13
other	3
Total	16

Le Mans 1949. Two body styles on the Two-Litre Sports. Number 29 is Lawrie's privately entered drophead, while 28 is the Marcébal/Mathieson works saloon.

Chapter Four

The DB2

DB2 chassis. The racing tyres indicate that it is intended for a works competition car. Note the vertically paired side rails, to give increased bending strength in the centre. Also visible is the coil spring rear suspension.

It was no coincidence that the announcement of the new model in the British motoring press, in April 1950, occurred just as the New York Motor Show was about to open. Although sales in Great Britain and continental Europe would always be important, there was no doubting the company's determination to increase sales in North America as rapidly as possible. Only in this way could they reach the sales volume necessary not only to survive but also to fund the racing programme which was an essential aid to survival.

Although at first glance the DB2 closely resembles the prototype LML/49/4, it differs in a great many details. Importantly it is larger in both width and

headroom, and this has implications for both the chassis and the body. Although the shorter 8ft 3in wheelbase of the Le Mans cars is retained, the chassis is some five inches wider. There is now diagonal crossbracing both amidships and at the rear, and the sill area is strengthened by a third tube structure five inches vertically above the outermost member. This makes the chassis immensely resistant to bending stresses at its mid-point, and allows the upper part of the framework aft of the door opening to be dispensed with. The forward structure forming the engine compartment and supporting the boxed scuttle and bulkhead is retained; the bulkhead itself is of double-skin construction and filled with glass wool to minimise transmission of both noise and heat from the engine.

The remaining points of the chassis design are largely unchanged from the Two-Litre Sports. Front suspension is independent using the same coil-spring and trailing-arm system, including the oil-filled casting, containing the transverse anti-roll bar, which lubricates the suspension pivots and the steering centre-pivot. Rear suspension is also by coil springs but non-independent, using semi-trailing arms and a Panhard rod. Suspension movement is five inches at the front and seven at the rear; the effect of the Panhard rod is to raise the rear roll-centre to just below the axle line, whereas at the front it is at ground level. Compared with the Two-Litre Sports the rear axle ratio is higher, at 3.77:1 in place of 4.1:1, although the old ratio was still available to special order. With the higher ratio a buyer could specify a close-

The right side of the engine, showing the complex exhaust manifolding.

ratio gear-set with uprated second and third, although this was only available with the optional central gearchange and not with the column-mounted change. The 19-gallon fuel tank has a three-gallon reserve with a solenoid-operated switch, and feeds through twin SU electric pumps.

With the removal of the upper framework at the rear of the chassis, it is now necessary for the body to be self-supporting. This is achieved firstly by using the steel sills and rear wheel arches as integral parts of the body structure, and secondly by constructing a separate lightweight framework to support the roof and tail. This is formed from Z-section steel with small-diameter tubing welded to it, and is attached to the chassis via four Silentbloc mountings. The edges of the aluminium panels are then turned round this frame, making them partially stressed components and adding to the rigidity of the body. The increase in headroom is some four inches, and the windscreen is increased in depth correspondingly. As with the Le Mans cars, the bonnet and front wings form a single

structure which is hinged at its forward edge, and which when opened gives superb access to the engine, front suspension, battery and tools. Provision is made for the hinge-pins themselves to be quickly detachable, to permit even better access during servicing.

As far as potential customers were concerned, the major point of interest was the new six-cylinder 78 x90mm engine, although it was of course already familiar to Lagonda owners. As we have already seen, its two most unusual features are firstly that it has wet liners, and secondly that it has a barrel-type cast-iron crankcase in which the crankshaft complete with main bearings and housings is inserted from the rear. However there are many other points of interest, starting with the valves themselves. It is said that the engine is designed around its valves, and it is true to the extent that in order to achieve the required port areas the resultant inclined valve arrangement and hemispherical combustion chamber were virtually a foregone conclusion. The valves are arranged at

an included angle of 60°, and the twin overhead camshafts operate directly on them through cast-iron bucket tappets on the ends of the valve stems. Inlet and exhaust valves have diameters of 1⅜in and 1¼in respectively, and they operate in a cast-iron head with hardened cast-iron inserts. The 10mm spark plugs are positioned vertically between the two rows of valves.

The design gives a minimum inertia of moving parts, which coupled with the fact that the camshafts each have 12 bearings leads to both reduced wear and quieter operation. The camshafts are driven from the front of the crank-shaft by a two-stage arrangement of duplex chains, with the water-pump shaft common to both upper and lower chains. A third chain, again taken from the front of the crankshaft, takes a separate drive to the distributor and oil pump. There are tensioners on the two camshaft drive chains, using hydraulic pressure – a change from the blade-type tensioners on the original Lagonda design. Another necessary change was to the fan drive, which on

Wheel-changing tools are held under the bonnet, on the side of the scuttle.

the Lagonda engine was mounted on an auxiliary sprocket driven by the upper camshaft chain. This positioned the fan blades too high above the engine, and the DB2 fan has a separate spindle cast lower down in the timing cover and shares a belt drive with the dynamo. For the time being the former fan-drive sprocket merely idles, although later it was to be designed out.

Since the cylinders are in the form of wet liners, there is no cylinder block as such, the barrel crankcase and cylinder water jackets extending upwards to the head joint line. The liners, of centrifugally cast iron, are sealed at the bottom with Hallite – sometimes known as Klingerite – washers and at the top by the cylinder head gasket. Hallite, a kind of fibrous steam gasket, was soon to be replaced by copper; both are in the form of "figure-of-eight" gaskets sealing pairs of liners. The

View of left side of the Aston Martin engine.

The crankshaft with three of the main bearings in position, and the crankcase, showing the circular registers for the main bearing housings or "cheeses".

crankshaft is a four main bearing design, sufficiently stiff and compact not to require a damper. While its front bearing is fixed in the crankcase, the three remaining bearings and their alloy housings are assembled to the crankshaft in advance and the whole assembly is then threaded into place from the rear. The bearing material is white metal backed with steel, whereas that for the big ends is a thin (0.30in) coating of white metal run directly into the steel. The H-section steel connecting rods are unusual in having their big-end bolts forged integrally and subsequently machined. At the small end the pistons are connected via bronze bushes and fully-floating gudgeon pins with circlips; the pistons have four rings, all above the gudgeon pin, the upper two being compression rings and the lower two for oil control.

Oil circulation is via a full-flow filter to the main

bearings and thence through drillings in the crankshaft to the big ends. A separate pressure feed is taken via the camshaft chains and their tensioners through the camshafts to the camshaft bearings, and then to small reservoirs surrounding the tappets. As for cooling water, this is fed from the pump to the off (exhaust) side of the head and thence directly under each of the six exhaust ports to the valve seats and guides; there is also a secondary feed to the cylinder liners. At the top of the head, between the camshaft covers, there is a take-off for return water to the radiator via a thermostat. This take-off is modified from the standard Lagonda design to suit installation in the DB2, which has a lower header tank and hence less height available between engine and bonnet. On the induction side, twin manifolds each feed three inlet ports from two horizontal 1½in SU carburettors. With the standard 6.5:1 compression ratio this version of the engine produces 105bhp at 5000rpm.

As far as the interior of the car is concerned, one major change from the prototype is the increase in headroom and windscreen depth already mentioned. Another is the effect of the new upper chassis member, which makes the sills significantly higher and gives the impression that the seats are set lower in the car. The two seats themselves, although separate, are flat rather than shaped and fit close together, so that they are in effect a divided bench seat. The passenger seat is wider than the driver's and carries a folding armrest. Provided the seats are aligned, their combined width of 50 inches is sufficient to permit three

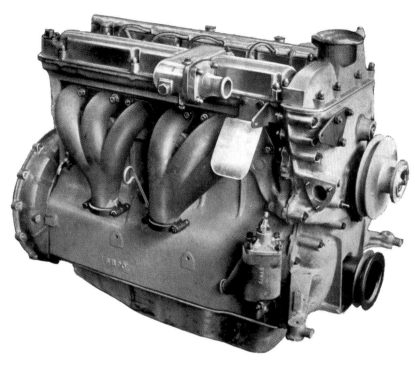

View of offside of the Aston Martin engine.

people to be carried in front, although this is only feasible in cars with the optional steering-column gearchange. Once again, the company persisted in the belief that the space behind the seats, reached by tipping the seat squabs forward, could be used for a fourth passenger instead of luggage, and even offered to fit an occasional seat there as an optional extra. A large spring steering wheel is fitted, with telescopic adjustment. The instrument panel is totally changed from the previous layout

The DB2's instrument panel is completely revised compared with that of the Two-Litre Sports.

This cutaway rendering of the DB2 shows how the pair of chassis side-rails resulted in a high internal sill which makes entry difficult.

The rear compartment is really intended for luggage, but it could accommodate a child for a short trip. The padded platform was an optional extra.

and now contains four separate round dials set symmetrically in the centre, with cubbyholes each side. The tachometer is closest to the driver, then comes a four-in-one gauge for engine-temperature, ammeter, oil-pressure and petrol/oil contents, then the speedometer (with inset clock) and furthest away the wipers, light switch, petrol reserve, starting and starting carburettor switch combined into one circular dial. A heater is fitted as standard – by no means a normal feature in those days – taking its air from a small domed inlet at the rear edge of the bonnet.

Externally one's eye is drawn to the large chromium grilles each side of the bonnet, replacing the former louvres. These grilles had by now become purely decorative, contributing

There are two separate seats which can be aligned to form a a bench ...

... and their backs fold down to give access to the rear compartment.

nothing to either engine cooling or brake cooling, and were soon to disappear. Also noticeable are twin flaps at the rear, unlocked from inside the car, which conceal quick-action fuel fillers. There is no access from outside to the luggage compartment, but there is a small door set low in the tail concealing the spare wheel, which is held in place by a neat over-centre clamp. The large, slightly curved rear window is made from Perspex, as are the rear quarter-windows. At the front the three-piece grille of the prototype is continued, but the centre section is necessarily taller than that of the previous year's Le Mans cars. A chrome rubbing strip runs round the car at hub level, picking up the line of the front bumper and functioning as the rear bumper. The 16in wheels fitted greatly

DB2 LML/50/5 when new. It has an early grille design, modelled on the drophead DB1.

Works car LML/50/7 is still an early version with bonnet grilles and all-round rubbing-strip, but the central grille has been modified with fewer bars.

improved the stance of the car, but 18in ones were said to be available for owners who wanted to raise the overall gearing still further.

The Autocar summed up the car as one which "will appeal to the connoisseur who likes long-distance high speed driving, or to the business man who must cut travelling time to the minimum, and it will still be suitable for competition use when required". *The Motor* commented on the car's "extraordinarily pleasing lines", and on the "handsome walnut facia panel … the finest quality leather is used for the upholstery and this applies also to the woodwork and trimmings." British Aston Martin enthusiasts by now had their tongues

hanging out, but they had to wait a little longer, as all attention was being focussed on the North American launch. The centrepiece was the New York Show, and its success was apparent when the company announced the next month (May) that total orders received for the "Aston-Martin-Lagonda division" during the Show totalled $70,000 – a worthwhile sum in those days, and probably representing about 100 cars. From surviving records it is obvious that the vast majority of the early production run went overseas. Out of the first 40 production cars only three stayed in Britain, and of the remainder 16 – approaching one half – went to North America. Some famous motoring names appeared on the list of early buyers, including Phil Hill and Briggs Cunningham; the latter bought two DB2 saloons from the first 20 sold, the second being fitted with the Vantage engine.

To maintain the interest of potential buyers both at home and abroad, the company resumed its racing programme for the 1950 season. Brown decided that he needed a permanent Racing Manager, and brought in John Wyer in what was to prove a long relationship with Aston Martin. Wyer had been apprenticed at the old Sunbeam company in Wolverhampton, then moved to Solex carburettors, and then to Monaco Garage in Watford, becoming managing director. Monaco specialised in preparing private entrants' cars for competition, but when the garage became a Vaux-

hall dealership Wyer lost interest. Brown had seen the methodical way in which Wyer had run a pit at Spa in 1948, and decided to snap him up.

Wyer entered three cars – LML/50/7, /8 and /9 – for that year's Le Mans, driven by Charles Brackenbury/Reg Parnell, George Abecassis/Lance Macklin and Jack Fairman/Eric Thompson. These became a famous trio of team cars, with consecutive registrations VMF 63, VMF 64 and VMF 65. Work on preparing the cars did not begin until 1 March, and in the time available Wyer could only make minor modifications to the previous year's model. These included some engine tuning and the substitution of Alfin brake drums in an attempt to improve the deterioration in brake performance which the team had experienced the year before.

Bad luck struck again, this time even before the race had started, when the Fairman/ Thompson car, being driven to the circuit by Fairman with his pregnant wife as passenger, was involved in an accident late at night and was too badly damaged to repair in time. The spare car – LML/49/3, UMC

66 (one of the previous year's team cars) – was substituted, and since Fairman had not recovered fully he was replaced by John Gordon. Thereafter things went quite well for the team. Although the older car understandably proved unable to last the course, the other two finished fifth and sixth overall and first and second in their class. The leading car, of Abecassis and Macklin, also tied for first place on handicap (the Index of Performance). *The Autocar*'s sporting editors commented, "Of the British cars which did so well, the Aston Martins, in particular, put up a fine performance in the best tradition of the marque. It was good to see a properly organised British team competing seriously and achieving results, and again the organisation was excellent". David Brown was so pleased that he asked John Wyer, who had only been engaged on a one-year contract, to join the company on a permanent basis, with the title of Chief Development Engineer.

The three team cars, VMF 64 having been repaired, were then entered for the one-hour

The body shop at Feltham - DB2s and Lagondas together

More shots of chassis LML/50/109
Above: The bonnet side-grilles had also long disappeared by this time.

Right: A flap in the rear wing opens to reveal the petrol filler.

Far right: There are chrome strips to the scuttle air-intake.

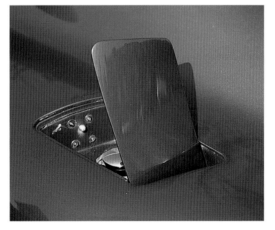

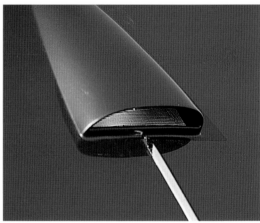

production car race at Silverstone, where the drivers were Parnell, Thompson and the French star Raymond Sommer, standing in for Macklin who had hurt his foot. Sommer came in second in the three-litre class, and apologised for not winning. Next came the Tourist Trophy race at Dundrod, near Belfast. This was the first TT since the war, and it attracted great interest, particularly since two Jaguar XK120s were also entered, driven by Stirling Moss and Peter Whitehead. The DB2 drivers were Abecassis, Parnell and Macklin, and the cars were of course in a smaller-engined class

than the Jaguars. In this class – up to three litres – they took the first three places, Parnell in VMF 63 coming first followed by Abecassis in VMF 65 and Macklin in VMF 64. In the overall placings, which were calculated on a handicap formula, the cars came in fourth, fifth and eighth. The three-hour race was run in a steady downpour which reduced wear and tear on tyres and brakes, but even so Macklin's car suffered some brake problems which contributed to his lower placing.

The autumn of 1950, and the approaching Motor Show, saw what was in effect the British launch of

Above: There are chrome strips on the bonnet, above each headlamp.

Above left: Trim strips around the vee-windscreen had been deleted by the time production reached this chassis number.

When the one-piece bonnet is tipped forwards, the rectangular tubing of the chassis is clearly visible.

Aston Martin lost no time in advertising their 1950 Le Mans success.

ASTON MARTIN
wins at Le Mans!

1st and 3rd in Fourth Annual Cup

3-litre lap record

1st and 2nd in 3-litre class

3-litre total distance record
(subject to official confirmation)

the DB2, with the basic price (before the vagaries of purchase tax) held at £1498 as for the DB1. First came a road test by *The Motor*, who decided to drive it round continental Europe for 1000 miles – an unusually high test mileage for those days. The particular car was VMF 63 (chassis LML/50/7), one of the famous trio of works cars. The test was carried out only three days after the car had taken part in a Production Car race at Silverstone, and it was delivered to the magazine still on its racing tyres. These were deemed responsible for exaggerating the shake which the testers experienced on rough roads (and since they were in Belgium they probably meant the notorious "pavé"), and for rattles coming from the bonnet stay and number plate. These were a few of many minor niggles which the testers found it necessary to mention, and this in an era when it was still thought somewhat impolite to criticise a new car which a manufacturer had been kind enough to lend. Nevertheless they were clearly impressed overall; their attitude was, "If [the car] falls short of perfection in some aspects, it has also such exceptional major virtues that the shortcomings may be forgiven even if they are not overlooked entirely". They then further blunted their criticism by adding that "the manufacturers are completely justified in refusing to delay production until every rattle or

other minor defect has been eliminated".

The concept of a high-performance closed car was still something of a novelty: "The latest six-cylinder Aston Martin ... may well presage a new era of sports cars combining unprecedentedly high performance with many of the amenities of the normal closed car". The testers pointed out the main advantage of a closed car over an open one in this respect, which was a marked reduction in air resistance, meaning that for the same power it could attain a significantly higher maximum speed. At the same time it could be used as everyday business transport, with little weight penalty compared with its open equivalent. They also welcomed the advanced nature of its design, "whereas most of the cars with which it may be compared are old-established designs which have been developed within their limits to a high pitch of perfection".

After the meagre diet of small family saloons which had come their way in postwar Britain, the testers obviously enjoyed to the full the opportunity to evaluate the qualities of the DB2. "Speed and roadworthiness of a high order" was their verdict, and indeed they managed to wring out of it some remarkable figures. However their rapture had to be modified some six weeks later when they slipped into their news pages (under the

The small rear window is a quick identification point for the DB2.

with the standard engine. The maximum speed, however, was another matter; the testers recorded a best one-way figure of 117.3mph, which is likely to be some 10mph faster than a standard car could have achieved.

There were other niggles, some of them serious. Although in general the car's cornering behaviour, and especially its lack of roll, came in for high praise, there was comment on its stability at high speed. "It is not hard to hold the car true on its course but it requires more conscious driving than do some modern types." This might not mean much in itself, but it is significant in the light of similar – and more serious – comments from the American driver Tom McCahill the following year. A noisy exhaust system also came in for criticism, as did the weak horn note and, particularly, inadequate lights. The strongest words were reserved for the brakes, which apparently began satisfactorily and then steadily deteriorated. This last phenomenon is surprising in a competition car, and one is left to surmise that the brakes had not been properly checked over after the Silverstone race.

The next piece of news in the build-up to the Motor Show was the unveiling of the DB2's drophead version. Pictures published in the motoring press showed VMF 37 (chassis LML/50/10), the prototype drophead which was to become David Brown's personal transport. Its appearance followed closely that of the saloon, down to wind-down windows and hinged quarter-lights. When folded the hood was not totally concealed, but under its neat cover it broke the line of the tail only slightly. There was still no separate boot access, luggage being stowed by folding down the seat backs as in the saloon.

Around the time of the Motor Show the uprated "Vantage" engine, numbered LB6V instead of LB6B, became officially available. This had its

heading "Aston Martin Prices") the admission that the road test car had in fact been fitted with the higher-powered "Vantage" engine – the existence of which had been hinted at in the initial publicity. This raised the basic price of the car by £100 and the tax-paid total to £2042. As against this, the car was fitted with the "largest available size of tyre and wheel", namely 6.00 x 16 instead of 5.75 x 16 (any thought of fitting 18in wheels seems to have been abandoned); also, as we have seen, it had the close-ratio gearbox. This combination will have taken the edge off the acceleration in the intermediate gears, and one might therefore say that *The Motor*'s recorded acceleration times up to the third gear maximum of 90mph – 25.1 seconds – would roughly equate to those of a normally-geared car

The DB2's roof slopes downward at the rear much more sharply than on the later DB2/4 models.

compression ratio raised from the standard 6.5:1 to 8.16:1, which together with larger carburettors (1¾in instead of 1⅛in) gave a useful increase in power output from 105bhp to 125bhp. Later versions of the Vantage engine (VB6B) had induction manifolds of increased size which produced no significant increase in power but gave a smoother delivery of the available performance.

Just to complicate matters, there were a few intermediate Vantage variants (LB6E) with the larger carburettors and induction manifold but a compression ratio of 7.5:1, producing 116bhp. A Vantage engine was on display on the Aston Martin stand, together with two examples of the DB2, a saloon and a drophead coupé. At the same time the company announced that since production

There are those who think that the DB2, especially from this angle, is the most stylish of all Feeley's postwar designs.

Once again, no outside coachbuilder was involved.

DB2 chassis number LML/50/10 was the first drophead coupé built, and became David Brown's personal car.

started it had increased the size of the front brake drums, which were now 2¼in wide, increasing the lining area from 152 to 172sq in.

Next in what must have been a planned programme of publicity was a road test by *The Motor's* great rival, *The Autocar*. This used another of the team cars, VMF 65 (chassis LML/50/9), which this time had the standard 105bhp engine with the 6.5:1 compression ratio; like its brother VMF 63 it wore 6.00 x 16 wheels. The reduction in performance was clear, although more in terms of maximum speed than acceleration. Acceleration times from rest to 60 and 90mph respectively were 12.4secs and 27.2secs, compared with 11.2secs and 25.1secs from VMF 63, while the maximum speed achieved was only 110mph against 117mph. Nevertheless the team of testers judged the car to be "in the first rank for handling and sheer brilliance of performance". Not to be outdone by *The Motor*, they covered 1900 miles in 10 days and clearly enjoyed the experience, including reaching 96mph in third gear, which meant 5750rpm against a "recommended" maximum of 5000.

The car had taken part in the Tourist Trophy event some three weeks prior to the test and was still on the harder competition damper settings.

This no doubt accounts for some criticism of suspension harshness over poorer surfaces, although it must also have contributed to the car's stability and accurate steering during fast cornering, which came in for praise. There were other criticisms: the exhaust note was too loud, the driver's seat lacked lateral support, the twin horns were weak for a fast car and the same applied to the lights. More seriously, the testers experienced pedal judder and "front end vibration" when braking from high speed, although significantly no sign of brake fade. It would appear that the Alfin drums fitted to the team cars were doing the right job for a competition car, but perhaps not for a businessman's express. The judder was later traced to drum ovality.

Next to test the car was the magazine *Motor Sport*, and in the diehard spirit typical of that journal's staff they decided to try the new drophead coupé in the middle of the 1950-51 winter. This was chassis LML/50/10 (VMF 37), the Show exhibit which had become David Brown's personal car. One factor immediately noticeable about the drophead is that – if the published figures are comparable – its weight is substantially less than that of the saloon, at "approximately 22cwt"

(2460lbs/1120kg) compared with 2662lbs (1207kg) for the saloon. This tells us how much the roof structure contributes to the overall weight, and also that, unlike with modern dropheads, there has been no additional reinforcement to compensate for the removal of the fixed roof and frame. However the performance figures do not support the weight loss theory, the drophead coupé accelerating slightly more slowly at 12.7secs for the 0-60mph dash as against 12.4secs with *Autocar*'s otherwise similar saloon (*The Motor* in their Vantage-engined car achieved 11.2secs.) Top speeds were effectively identical at 109 and 110mph. *Motor Sport*, not surprisingly, experienced appalling weather during their test, which may have affected the performance figures.

Motor Sport's testers were, like every other magazine's, bowled over by the totally non-vintage behaviour of this unconventional car. "It is difficult to believe that this softly sprung, seemingly very wide motor car will handle safely at high speeds, while so effortlessly does it accelerate that one is deceived into thinking that the acceleration is only modest. When derestricted roads are reached first impressions need to be hastily revised, for the handling qualities are really superb and the more

remarkable because the car is so well sprung, while very few automobiles will reach the seventies, eighties and nineties so rapidly and unobtrusively." They particularly liked its "well-nigh perfect cornering and roadholding characteristics", including the "slight understeer that denotes pedigree", summarising the car in this respect as one of the safest they had ever tested. The suspension also met with their approval, leaving them wondering at the combination of soft springing with such "splendid" roadholding. Even the brakes came in for compliments, tending to confirm that they were at least capable of standing up to normal road use.

Criticisms were few. The bench front seat would take two slim passengers beside the driver "providing they knew each other reasonably well", the dashboard layout was confusing, and the design of the grilles on the bonnet sides – which they thought, erroneously, had some purpose in extracting air – was such that "the vulgar might be tempted to strike matches" on them. Although the steering-column gearchange which came with the car behaved well, the testers would have preferred the floor-mounted version. Interestingly, the exhaust note escaped criticism, which might not be

unconnected with the car having a soft, non-resonating roof. The overall summary was that the DB2 offered "the performance, stability and joy-of-handling associated with the sports/racing car while remaining a completely docile, comfortable, practical and withal economical high-grade touring car"; in short, it was "one of the world's really great cars".

It must have been at about this time, early 1951, that someone at Feltham carried out a costing exercise on the DB2, because soon afterwards two things happened: the price went up, and a severe cost-reduction programme began. The price increase was substantial, with the basic prices of both the saloon and the drophead coupé moving up by £352, to £1750 and £1850 respectively (£2723 and £2879 with tax). The cost reductions involved such things as the removal of the decorative side grilles and of the sill-level rubbing strips (although the latter could still be ordered as an extra), and the deletion of one of the two fuel fillers. Furthermore the standard of interior trim became less elaborate, and out went such things as the plated brass strips for the windscreen surrounds and the rain gutters over the rear quarter-lights. These changes seem to have taken place around chassis numbers /49 to /51, which would date them to the April/May period in 1951. At about the same time chassis manufacture was moved from Feltham to David Brown's Farsley

works, presumably again to reduce costs.

From the company's point of view this sudden concentration on profitability – at least within the UK – came just in time, since deliveries to British customers had only just started. Up to December 1950 all cars had been exported, but on the 8th of that month a lucky Mr Johnson from Kent became the first UK owner of a new DB2 (although a few of the works cars had been sold secondhand). However it was not until the following February that the second such delivery took place – or the third if you include David Brown's own drophead. This slow rate of delivery can be attributed entirely to the necessity for all companies in those days to achieve a high export ratio, but the size of the price increase makes one wonder just how much latent demand there would have been for the car. It is therefore instructive to compare the DB2's new price with other cars of the same class available on the UK market.

If one defines the Aston Martin's market segment as high-quality, closed performance cars, and limits it further to those with a good postwar competition record, then the DB2 had very few direct competitors: the Healey Tickford saloon comes to mind immediately, as does the Allard P1 saloon. These were priced at the time (including purchase tax) at £2303 and £1945 respectively, and both had a good record in international competition in such events as Le Mans and the Monte Carlo Rally. On

The sporting Healey Tickford saloon, powered by the Riley twin-camshaft 2½-litre engine, was a competitor to the DB2 and was cheaper as well.

The Allard P1 saloon, another competitor, was even cheaper, and had a good record in rallies. This is Sidney Allard after winning the 1952 Monte Carlo Rally.

paper the Allard looked a strong rival, but its imported American engine meant that it lacked some appeal for the more technically-minded. Other, apparently obvious, competitors did not have a closed car to offer. The Jaguar XK120 fixed-head coupé, for example, did not appear until later in 1951, and the equivalent Frazer Nash not for another two years. Import restrictions meant that any car not assembled in Great Britain was out of bounds. Putting the question the other way round – what other cars could your Aston Martin money

A Ferrari 212, David Brown's most feared competitor, descending the Gavia Pass on the 1953 Alpine Rally.

buy? – might have suggested a Bristol 401 saloon (£3260) but not much else.

It is reasonable to conclude that within the UK the DB2 was under-priced at launch and that its subsequent price increase was justified by what the market would bear. In the important North American market, of course, entirely different rules applied. There the DB2 was up against the world's best, and the competitor which David Brown feared most was undoubtedly Ferrari with its combination of V12 mystique and competition success. This may well account for the relatively low price of $5000 (delivered to New York City) which he put on the car at its launch. Brown's New York Show debut with the car the previous year had done wonders in putting the marque on the map, and a year later the DB2 was the talk of the moneyed cognoscenti. Just when all seemed to be going well, however, a review of the car appeared in the American magazine *Mechanix Illustrated* which was distinctly unwelcome as far as the company were concerned. Written by the magazine's regular correspondent Tom McCahill, a

well-known "stock" (production) car driver, it called into question the DB2's claim to world-class roadholding.

It is clear that McCahill went into the test with some optimism: "Sophisticated journalists ... and starry-eyed car collectors ... have been so reckless in throwing around applause for the Aston that your Uncle Tom finally decided an investigation of the claims was in order". In Florida he borrowed Briggs Cunningham's Vantage-engined model and set it at one of the many straight but notoriously bumpy Everglades roads. At speeds above 100mph he reported that the steering became highly sensitive – dangerously so – and that he had to hang on to the steering-wheel hard with both hands to retain control. In a follow-up test he concluded that this combination of lightness at the front end and an oversteering tendency also affected the car's cornering, with the tyres retaining their grip to quite a high speed and then losing it suddenly. An equally experienced companion confirmed his findings.

McCahill's experience as a competition driver

showed through in his summing-up. "It [the DB2] seems to be poorly balanced. There is just a chance that the front ends, as delivered in this country, do not have the right caster and camber for fast running, causing them to duck-walk at top speed". As things turned out he had probably hit the nail on the head. Whereas the cars which had been offered for road test up to now in the UK were all works team cars, which had been the subject of a great deal of suspension tuning to optimise their handling, the Briggs Cunningham car was just a normal delivery to a private buyer. It seems that until this incident the works were unaware that the front suspension set-up was so sensitive to small differences in camber and caster angle – particularly caster. Probably it is more than coincidence that before long a modification would be introduced, using an eccentric pin in the upper trailing link to permit fine adjustment of caster.

Back in England another experienced motoring journalist was coming to a quite different conclusion. John Bolster of *Autosport* had the use of a DB2 for a few days and lost no time in treating the roads as a racetrack wherever possible. "I can say at once that it responds magnificently to the four wheel drift technique, and that even the most extreme methods fail to show up any tricks or vices. I remember one particular curve, which was wet and glistening with rain, through which I slid

under full control at just over the century." The difference was, of course, that he had again been given one of the works cars, VMF 65. By this time it would appear that the suspect braking of these cars had become more widely known, but also that the company had done something about it. "The brakes were always smooth and constant in action, and could be applied hard at maximum speed without any risk of deviation. No fierceness or grabbing was ever apparent, and it would appear that a very severe problem has now been overcome." Bolster quoted the lining area as 152sq in, but this figure would imply 2in wide front shoes whereas we know that by that time the width had increased to 2¼in.

Elsewhere the test report continued to use superlatives, the car having "impeccable" town manners and being "luxuriously appointed". Bolster even found that "no garish decoration mars the functional beauty of the aerodynamic body", overlooking the non-functional bonnet grilles and the sill rubbing-strips that were both about to disappear. He also produced some notable – one might say incredible – performance figures from a car which was stated to have had its Vantage competition engine removed and a standard 6.5:1 compression engine substituted. A 0-60mph acceleration time of 10.8secs was nearly two seconds faster than two other journals had managed in

The DB2's front suspension set-up was highly sensitive to caster angle.

Lord Brabazon, pioneer motorist and aviator, with his DB2 LML/50/88 - David Brown beside him.

ostensibly similar cars, and was faster than *The Motor* had managed with a Vantage engine. Admittedly engine development had continued in the intervening time, but one is inclined to question whether the car given to *Autosport* was exactly what the company claimed it to be – either that or someone's hand slipped on the stopwatch. "Best of all", proclaimed Bolster, "a British firm has at last broken the Italian monopoly in beautiful high-speed saloons."

While British buyers waited impatiently to be allowed the privilege of acquiring a DB2, such production as did leave the factory was going almost entirely overseas. There was nothing half-hearted about the company's export marketing programme. They had followed up the New York Show launch in 1950 with a similar stand at the Canadian National Fair in August/September of that year, and then continued in 1951 with appearances at Brussels, Melbourne, Paris and Turin. Some notable customers resulted, including Prince Bertil of Sweden. How many sales could be directly attributed to all this activity is hard to say, but the company must have thought it worthwhile

because they continued with further rounds of shows in 1952 (Amsterdam, Brussels, Geneva) and 1953 (Brussels, Lille, Paris).

There were other things going on at the factory besides production. John Wyer had concluded after the 1950 Le Mans that he was never going to win that event, or any other sports car race, merely by modifying the current production car – the "prototype clause" had seen to that. Aston Martin had admittedly taken advantage of that clause in 1949, when they ran a DB1 with the then non-standard 2.6 engine, but at least they had intended that it should go into production and indeed it did. Others, it was clear, were going to develop one-off "prototypes" specifically to win sports-car races, and that meant to Wyer that Aston Martin had to do the same. Accordingly in November of 1950 Dr Eberan von Eberhorst had arrived to start work at Feltham as Chief Engineer (thus becoming Wyer's immediate boss). His fame preceded him, for while he was working with Porsche before the war he had designed the 1938 D Type Auto Union grand prix car. Although Austrian by birth, he had found himself in East Germany at the end of the war and

escaped before the Russian occupation took hold. He took a post in Turin, working on the Porsche-designed Cisitalia flat-12 grand prix car, but there were financial problems with the project. When in 1948 his old friend Laurence Pomeroy visited him, it was obvious to Pomeroy that von Eberhorst would like to move, and Pomeroy was instrumental in arranging a position for him with ERA at their new location at Dunstable. However the facil-

A famous team car, XMC 76 (chassis LML/ 50/50) is seen in modern-day form prepared for racing; note the Perspex side-windows. It was one of the first with the one-piece radiator grille.

Above: The interior of XMC 76, lacking some interior trim in the interests of lightness.

Right: A 1951 works competition car straight off the production line.

The third team car at Le Mans, driven by Parnell and Hampshire, finished third in its class. Behind it is a 726cc Crosley Hot Shot.

ities there were rather primitive, and when the position at Feltham became available von Eberhorst was ready to move once again.

His brief from the company was nothing less than to design a sports-racer, new apart from the engine, as quickly as possible (and also a replacement for the Lagonda saloon, but that is another story). Even so, it was soon apparent to Wyer that the new car might not be available to him for the 1951 season, and as a precaution Wyer began work on improving the performance of the existing cars through severe weight reduction. This he carried out with his customary thoroughness, starting by deleting the trim and moving on through the seats, wheels and electrical system to the substitution of Perspex instead of glass (except for the windscreen) and 18-gauge aluminium instead of 16-gauge for the outer panels. This spec-

ification was applied firstly to two new works cars, LML/50/50 and /55, later registered XMC 76 and XMC 77 and driven by Abecassis/Shaw Taylor and Macklin/Thompson respectively. There was hope at that point that at least one new car, dubbed the DB3, would be ready in time. However, when it became clear that this was not going to happen, one of the previous year's cars, LML/50/8 (VMF 64), to be driven by Macklin/Thompson, was also converted within the time available to something close to the new specification, including the latest one-piece radiator grille. There were also at least two important mechanical upgrades: a twin exhaust system was fitted, and the two SU carburettors were replaced by three dual-choke Webers. When Macklin had tried out this latter modification at the Weber factory on the way to take part in the Targa Florio the previous year he had noted a

The Abecassis/Shaw Taylor car (LML/50/55) at Arnage during the 1951 Le Mans, alongside an 851cc D.B. driven by Bonnet/Bayol.

The 1951 Le Mans winner was a C-type Jaguar driven by Peter Walker, seen here at Tertre Rouge.

Another Le Mans entry in 1951 was a 3.8-litre Nash-engined Healey, which finished sixth driven by Rolt/Hamilton.

significant lift in power, although with some loss of smooth running. At the factory the two changes together lifted power output from 125bhp to 138. This in turn permitted the fitting of a higher rear axle ratio at 3.27:1.

Wyer used the opportunity of the Silverstone production car race, some six weeks before Le Mans, to test some of these changes. He knew he could not get the Webers past the scrutineers, but the cars managed to race with various other test components, including aluminium cylinder heads and revised inlet timing. The former did not prove a success, and the test also showed up gearbox problems which meant a completely new design had to be produced at very short notice. Incidentally the cars, with oil and water, weighed 2126lbs (964kg), which would appear to confirm Wyer's later claim that his programme had saved 450lbs (204kg).

Three private entries for the 1951 Le Mans were also prepared at the works: LML/50/57 (MKC 306) for Peter Clark, /59 (PPJ 2) for Nigel Mann and /64 (LXY 703) for Maurice Falkner; in the event the latter was only a reserve for the race and did not

take part. For the other five, however, it was something of a triumph, the three works cars taking the first three places – in the order Macklin, Abecassis, Parnell – in the three-litre class and the two privateers coming in at five and six. The works cars also achieved third, fifth and seventh places overall, against a host of larger-engined cars: first was a C-Type Jaguar, second and fourth were 4½-litre Talbots, and sixth was a Healey with the 3.8-litre Nash engine.

In an enlightened piece of public relations, the company allowed *The Autocar* a short drive in VMF 64 in its Le Mans specification immediately after it returned to England. This car was fast becoming something of a legend, having won its class in two successive Le Mans and in the meantime produced a class win in private hands (Tommy Wisdom and Tony Hume) in the Mille Miglia. It would go on to distinguish itself in two Alpine trials and another Mille Miglia. Even though British roads in those days had no overall speed limit, neither were there any motorways, so there was no opportunity to check the car's maximum

George Abecassis in typical pose in a sports-car race.

Chassis LML/50/69, a drophead coupé by Graber of Switzerland. This was the first of six Aston Martin chassis bodied by this firm.

speed, which was thought to be approaching 130mph. However, the journal recorded an approximate acceleration time from standstill to 100mph of 28-29 seconds, which compared with 38.8 seconds for the standard car. The writer described the acceleration as "the nearest thing to jet fighter performance likely to be vouchsafed to most of us here below".

As far as the company was concerned the major news in the autumn was the first appearance of the DB3 sports-racing car, at the Ulster Tourist Trophy event. As for the DB2, the Earls Court Show came and went. On the Aston Martin stand, in addition to the expected saloon (LML/50/52, XHX 26) and drophead coupé, there was a bare chassis. The company, hard at work on satisfying export orders and developing the DB3, had nothing new to proclaim. One might have expected the British coachbuilding fraternity to have welcomed an expensive car with a separate chassis such as the DB2, providing as it did another opportunity for them to show what they could do, but none had taken the plunge. This was certainly not the case

on the Continent, where the first of three chassis-only cars had already been supplied to Graber of Switzerland to turn into his own interpretation of a drophead coupé; a total of five cars were supplied in this form during the DB2's production run.

Soon afterwards, in the December issue of the American magazine *Road & Track*, there appeared an article which must have brought considerable relief to the company. This was a road test by the magazine's staff of a standard 6.5:1 saloon owned by Phil Hill, already a highly respected sports-car driver and later to become a Ferrari grand prix driver and world champion. Both the testers' comments and those of Hill himself make it clear that the car's handling was beyond reproach – a radical change since the notorious McCahill test earlier in the year. The magazine described it as "one of the best handling and fastest cars ever tested by the *Road and Track* staff", and they were also complimentary about its appearance: "a wonderful combination of British craftsmanship and coachwork combined with a shrewdly contrived envelope body". They achieved a two-

Tommy Wisdom and VMF 64, on their way to winning an Alpine Cup in the 1951 Alpine Rally.

1952 Berne Grand Prix: Geoff Duke's DB2 LML/50/55 is ahead of the Mercedes SL. Duke finished fourth.

way average top speed of 105.7mph, but surprisingly took no acceleration figures. Hill himself was equally enthusiastic – understandably, since he had bought the car with his own money. "The Aston handles as well as any sports car I've driven, far better than any normal passenger car … The DB2 handles like a dream and is a lot of fun to drive". Putting things in perspective, this was the era of the softly-sprung American barge, and Feltham would have been disappointed if their car had not handled better than anything of that ilk. Nevertheless Hill was familiar with the handling of sports cars set up for track use, and his comments carried weight. Importantly, they seemed to confirm that the handling quirks which McCahill had discovered had now been eliminated.

In May 1951 the motoring journalist Tommy

Wisdom had persuaded David Brown to lend him his personal DB2 to enter the Mille Miglia. To the surprise of Wyer and the racing department, Wisdom had driven magnificently to finish eleventh overall and win the Grand Touring class. This had caused Wyer to have a rethink, and he decided to put in a "reconnaissance" entry for the 1952 event. The team consisted of the two lightweight DB2s for Parnell and Abecassis and the older version, VMF 64, for Wisdom. To everyone's delight Wisdom repeated his previous year's performance, winning the GT class and pushing Parnell into second place by a mere two minutes; overall the two cars were placed twelfth and thirteenth. Abecassis experienced clutch failure after only 200km and retired. The two lightweight cars were also entered in the 1952 Prix de Berne, where Geoff Duke finished fourth and Parnell fifth behind three Mercedes 300SLs; Duke won the 500cc motorcycle event there on the same day.

When Motor Show time came around that year, 1952, there were very few changes to report in the DB2's specification. About the only piece of news was that the brake drums and shoes had been widened further, taking the lining area out to 191sq ins. On the Show stand were two drophead coupés – one right-hand drive, the other left-hand – and two saloons. One of the latter was standard except for the optional 2.6 Vantage engine, and the other was VMF 64 in its Mille Miglia livery. Of course the spotlight that year was on the first show appearance of the DB3, and parts of that car's development programme were already trickling down to the DB2. Amongst these was a prototype three-litre engine, which was fitted to a very few DB2s starting at this period. At about the same time a modification was implemented which the 2.6-litre engine had needed desperately since the DB2's launch. This was the

removal of the redundant idler sprocket in the secondary timing drive, which was originally used to drive the fan, and which had contributed nothing other than to shorten the life of the chain tensioner.

The DB2 had by now already gained its place in history; 411 examples of this hand-built car had been produced, the great majority for export. But what was to become of the works cars – the famous trio of VMF 63/4/5? For a time it seemed as if the company was reluctant to let them go, and they continued in various roles as personal staff cars, occasionally lent out to trusted drivers for competitions. Motoring journalists were not immune from the sentimentality which had built up. John Cooper, sports editor of *The Motor*, felt compelled to borrow VMF 64, the most famous of the three, one more time at the end of 1954. He added the car to the magazine's retrospective "Talking of Sports Cars" series, and wrote about it affectionately as of an old friend. It was not until two years later that the company sold off the three cars; even then they ensured that the trio all went to "good homes".

VMF 64, in Mille Miglia livery, takes pride of place on the Aston Martin stand at the 1952 Earls Court Show.

DB2 – Summary Statistics

Engine

configuration	6 cylinders in line, overhead valves, twin overhead camshafts
capacity	2580cc
bore	78mm
stroke	90mm
RAC rating	22.6hp
compression ratio	6.5:1 (Vantage: 8.16:1)
firing order	153624
valve timing	io 18° atdc,
tappet clearances (cold)	inlet .011-.013in, exhaust .012-.014in
brake horsepower	105 @ 5000rpm (Vantage: 120bhp)
crankshaft	
no of bearings	4
main bearing	2½in (63.5mm) diameter
big end	2in (51mm) diameter
crankcase capacity	15 pints (8.5 litres)
cooling system	water pump, thermostat bypass, capacity 3 galls (13.6 litres)
ignition details	Lucas B12 coil, 12 volts
ignition timing	5° btdc
contact breaker gap	.012in
plugs – make/gap	KLG L30 (Vantage: KLG P10 L80) 10mm/ .022in
carburettors	Twin 1½in SU H4 (Vantage: twin 1¾in SU)
fuel pump	Twin SU Type L electric
dynamo	Lucas C45 PVS-5
starter motor	Lucas M 45 G
clutch	Borg & Beck single plate type 9A6G
engine number location	Front of timing cover (OR on offside front bearer arm)

Gearbox

type	David Brown 4-speed
gear ratios	Steering-column change: 3.77, 5.02, 7.48 and 11.03 to 1; reverse 11.03:1. Central gear-change: 3.77, 4.75, 7.05 and 11.03 to 1
oil capacity	3 pints (1.7 litres)

Chassis

wheelbase	99in (2515mm)
track	54in (1372mm)
length	162½in (4128mm)
width	65in (1651mm)
weight (dry)	2464lb (1117kg)
turning circle	32ft (9.75m)
suspension	independent at front, live axle at rear, coil springs all round
wheels and tyres	Dunlop centre-lock wires, 5.75 or 6.00 x 16in
tyre pressures	26psi front, 27psi rear (30/31psi for high speed driving)
brakes	Girling 2LS hydraulic, drums 12in diameter
steering box	Marles worm and double roller
propeller shaft	open, Hardy Spicer
rear axle	hypoid bevel, Salisbury
ratio	3.77:1
oil capacity	2 pints (1.1 litres)
shock absorbers	Armstrong piston-type hydraulic
petrol tank capacity	19 galls (86 litres), incl. 3 galls (14 litres) reserve
chassis number location	Offside front of frame AND on bulkhead plate

Prices (excl. purchase tax)

saloon	1950: £1498. 1951: £1750
drophead coupé	1950: £1598. 1951: £1850

Numbers produced

saloon	308
drophead coupé	98
other	5
Total	411

Chapter Five

The DB2/4

Even while the DB3 prepared to make its mark in competition, and the design department pursued longer term projects such as the next Lagonda and a V12 engine, it must have been obvious that the DB2 was paying everyone's salaries and that its sales appeal should therefore be enhanced in every way possible. The car's biggest limitation in the market was the fact that it could only carry two people, or three at a tight squeeze; uprating it to a four-seater would open many new selling opportunities. Accordingly, some time in the winter of 1952-53, work began on a revision to the DB2 which would permit two reasonably comfortable seats to be installed at the rear.

The brief was easier to write than to execute. In that space was a clutter of petrol tank, spare wheel and – most crucial of all – chassis crossbracing. This was not of course the main bracing under the cabin floor, but some subsidiary struts which designer Ted Cutting had added when he was strengthening the somewhat flabby chassis of the DB1. In the end it proved possible to substitute a substantial new, right-angle crossmember, gusseted to the side rails. This both removed the obstruction behind the front seats and left a shallow rectangular space at the back for a new petrol tank. In the forward space went two vestigial but surprisingly comfortable seats, and to the rear went a very flat fuel tank, virtually within the depth of the side chassis members, holding 17 gallons in place of the former 19. The spare wheel was moved down to a hinged carrier below the tank.

And so was born the DB2/4, the designation

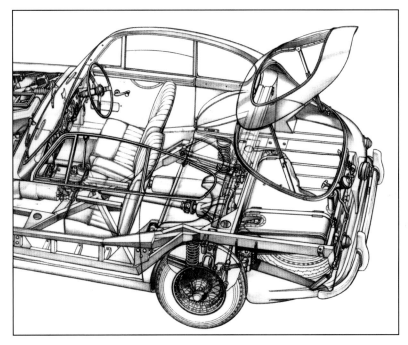

implying that the model now had four seats. These days it would probably be described as a "2+2", the seats being adequate to accommodate two adults for shorter journeys but perfectly satisfactory for carrying two children for long distances. This alone makes the car a practical proposition as a family car, but its attraction is enhanced by the additional luggage space which has been released. Furthermore Frank Feeley had a brainwave and, while enlarging the rear window, made the whole of the window and its frame into a door which lifts

For the DB2/4 the diagonal rear bracing at the rear of the chassis has been removed; a reinforced crossmember in front of the petrol tank has taken its place.

relocation of the spare wheel and the low height of the petrol tank, and can be increased by lowering the backs of the rear seats.

There were other changes to the bodywork, some of which were introduced with the prototype and others only at the time of the official launch just before the 1953 Earls Court Show. From the beginning there was a one-piece curved wind-screen, the roof line was raised compared with the car's predecessor in order to give more headroom at the back, and there was also a change to a more conventional style of bumper with overriders added. (Their method of attachment now meant, reassuringly, that only the bumper was damaged in a light collision rather than the whole front or back of the car.) The shape of the rear quarter-light was changed to blend in better with the new roof line; the same applied to the headlamps, which were raised in height for legislative reasons, necessitating a change to the shape of the bonnet. There were also revisions to the instrument panel, with the speedometer and tachometer now occupying the centre; the pedals were moved forward by two inches (50mm) to increase interior space; a telescopic steering-column was now specified; and the arm-rest between the seats now contained a fitted tool kit. Screen washers and a battery master

The interior can now accommodate two occasional rear seats. Seat backs fold down to give increased luggage space.

Feeley's masterstroke – the rear hatch, giving access to luggage. Rear roof height has been increased, and the rear quarter-light elongated. Note the single petrol filler.

upwards. This at last gives direct access to the luggage area, in the manner of a modern hatch-back. Feeley's design predates that trend by many years, and was also some six years ahead of a pioneer hatchback, the Austin A40 "Farina". The luggage space is of a useful size, thanks to the

Speedometer and tachometer are now in the centre of the instrument panel, but otherwise the layout is much the same as the DB2's.

The spare wheel is now carried below the petrol tank to create luggage space.

68 AMF (chassis LML 558) is a car which can hold up its head equally in either road-racing or concours d'elegance.

This car has non-standard chrome strips along the bonnet sides, a legacy of when it stood in for a Mark II when that model was launched.

switch were now standard fitments.

The other major change affecting the bodywork concerned manufacturing. No longer were Feltham to act as the Group's body shop, but instead body manufacture was contracted out to Mulliners of Birmingham. The trigger point for this decision, according to Frank Feeley, was the worsening state of labour relations at Feltham, which Feeley blamed on the recruitment of some former Weymann employees who held strong left-wing political views and who in furtherance of a pay dispute had even picketed the Huddersfield works. It was arranged that Mulliners would make the DB2/4 bodies from the outset, thus avoiding any

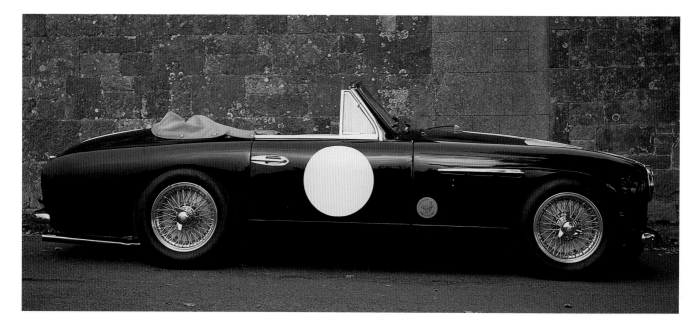

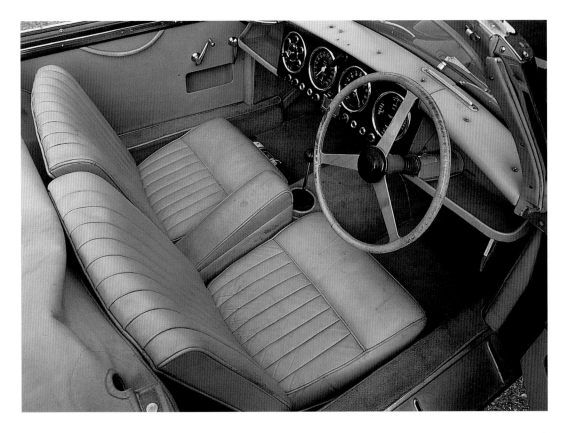

Separate front seats are standardised rather than the single bench type, but they share an arm-rest.

"handover" problems and giving the new supplier a clean start. Inevitably, however, things did not quite go to plan and Feeley found himself mediating between Mulliners and their own sub-contractors – primarily Airflow Streamlines of Northampton, who were doing the actual panel beating. (Mulliners by this time had presumably converted almost entirely to short-run presswork using Kirksite dies, but the small volumes from Aston Martin would not have justified even this investment.) Mulliners had no hand in the design of the new body, other than requesting a change from steel for the sills to a single aluminium casting for both sill and door pillar.

The front of the car is more upright than the DB2's, and the headlamps are mounted higher. The windscreen is now in one piece.

LML/762, one of the "Arnolt-Aston Martins" built by Italian coachbuilder Bertone for American importer "Wacky" Arnolt. This particular design is a drophead coupe.

In effect Mulliners were only an assembly operation for the bodies, followed by painting and trimming. Finished bodies – once passed by the resident inspector whom Feeley had felt obliged to install there – were transported to Feltham, there to meet up with the chassis and engines which had arrived from Yorkshire. Thus Feltham had itself become only an assembly shop, excepting of course the racing department which operated quite separately. One can begin to see that the whole precarious system was an accident waiting to happen – a delay in one small part of it would soon bring the whole operation to a close – and there is evidence that such a hold-up did in fact occur. It stems from a recent, and apparently mystifying, discovery: the first six production chassis were sent, as chassis only, to Italy.

There is no one still alive who is able to confirm what happened, but it seems likely that the sequence of events was as follows. The DB2/4 launch was probably planned for the spring of 1953, but for the reasons described above body production took much longer to get started than

had been expected. Meanwhile the David Brown Farsley factory was producing both chassis and engines according to the plan. Knowing that Italy was by then the centre of the world's coachbuilding industry, someone had the bright idea of exhibiting one of these chassis at the imminent Turin Show, in the hope that one or other coachbuilder there might be inspired to put bodies on it or even on a whole batch.

At this point we have to introduce the flamboyant American, Stanley H "Wacky" Arnold. Wacky

Bertone also created this stunning interior to match the striking coachwork.

Placing the coachbuilder's badge on the sides of the car was perfectly acceptable to the company but badging the car as an "Arnolt Aston Martin" certainly was not!

The heavy radiator grille is typical of Italian styling of the period.

Pimply rear lights were also much in fashion.

acquired his name through being the manufacturer of Waukesha marine engines, but by 1953 he had also become a major mid-West importer of British cars. Indeed he had gone further and in 1952 made an arrangement with the Italian firm Bertone to build coupé and convertible bodies on the MG TD chassis. During one short year 100 such cars were shipped to the States and sold as Arnolt-MGs; then Arnolt learned that the TD was to be superseded by the TF and that he was not going to be supplied with TF chassis. Thus it was that when he made his next visit to Turin, at the time of the 34th Salone dell'Automobile in April 1953, he was looking out for other chassis which Bertone could body for him. And what should he find but a brand-new Aston Martin chassis, begging to be bodied?

Some of the above is speculation, but only some. It is a fact that the first production chassis was sent to the 1953 Turin Show, and it is almost certain that Arnolt would have known he had lost the MG business by then. It is also a fact that the chassis in question, LML/503, acquired a Bertone body, although whether Arnolt was the customer in that particular case is unknown. The remaining fact is that the next five production chassis, LML/502 and /504-7, were built to left hand drive specification and sent to Bertone for bodying before being forwarded to Arnolt in the States. Thus the company's strategy could be said to have been highly successful in finding bodies for six chassis. Arnolt, however, could not resist the temptation to badge them as Arnolt Aston Martins. This upset the British company, which put a stop to his receiving any more chassis. (By that time the production hiccup had disappeared, for reasons we shall examine later). There was another mystery show chassis, LML/562, which was also bodied by Bertone, but not apparently for Arnolt. He somehow managed to obtain another two chassis later on (LML/762 and /765) but at that stage he was more concerned with his Arnolt Bristol project.

The supposition is therefore that the planned spring launch date for the DB2/4 had to be postponed until the autumn – in fact, just before the London Show. Production had been building gradually since June, and some 24 cars had been built before the launch date. This included the first car with a major change to the engine specification, although, mystifyingly, there was no announcement at the time. Prior to that point the standard specification had been the 2.6-litre Vantage engine, presumably because British fuel was now of a quality where it could take advantage of that engine's higher compression ratio. Now the capacity was changed to 2.9 litres as standard for the saloon, although the 2.6 engine remained as the standard fitting for the drophead coupé until April the following year. Interestingly, although the six Bertone cars were early ones fitted with 2.6-litre engines, by the time they were delivered to Arnolt's customers the 2.9 version had been substituted.

The redesign was in the hands of the engine's original designer, Willie Watson, who had been recruited back to the company mainly to take charge of the V12 Lagonda project. He decided to achieve the desired capacity increase by the apparently simple expedient of increasing the bore size from 78mm to 83mm. However there was insufficient distance between the bore centres to permit this without lengthening the engine, and the solution which the company adopted was to offset the bores alternately by 2.5mm about the centre-line of the crankcase. It was first decided to correct the resultant misalignment by offsetting the little-end bearing on the gudgeon pin, but a disastrous experience with the DB3s at the 1952 Monaco Grand Prix resulted in a redesign with the offset at the crankpin end. The production 2.9-litre engine, with a claimed power output of 140bhp, had first been announced with the launch of the Three-Litre Lagonda saloon in October 1953, but in fact it had been surreptitiously installed in the Aston Martin at the same time. When the motoring press were finally told about the increase in the DB2/4's engine capacity (in August 1954), it was stated that only models going to America had so far been fitted with the new engine, but that now it was being made available to the home market. All the evidence from factory records, however, is that once the bigger engine had been introduced it was standardised across the whole production run.

Arnolt-Bristol. "Wacky" Arnolt moved on to this project once his supplies of DB2/4 chassis dried up.

Why the announcement should have been delayed so long is a mystery, but it was possibly to ensure that dealers worldwide had cleared their stocks of the smaller-engined car.

Thus the new DB2/4 was revealed to British enthusiasts at the end of September 1953, with full descriptions in both *The Motor* of 30 September and *The Autocar* of 2 October, which also carried a full road test using the prototype car LML/50/221 (YMP 200), still wearing its wide-bar radiator grille. It would also appear from the performance figures that it had not yet received the 2.9-litre engine. In fact the 2.6 Vantage unit fitted did not produce any perceptible improvement in acceleration compared with the standard engine which the journal had tested previously in the DB2, thanks to a weight increase of some 110lb (50kg) which brought the bhp/ton figure to exactly where it had been. There was, however, some suggestion of an increase in maximum speed, with a one-way best of 120mph.

The new seats at the rear, and the increased luggage space, met with approval from both magazines. The testers from *The Autocar* noted that it

was necessary to tilt down the backs of the front seats to gain access, but that had not prevented them from carrying two extra adult passengers for 100 miles, apparently without excessive complaint. There were virtually no criticisms, apart from long clutch travel, and there were several compliments on the low level of noise from wind, body boom, engine and transmission, or transmitted from the road such as when running over cats-eyes. As before, there was high praise for the ride and road-holding. "Its cornering qualities at both high and low speeds are first rate, while general directional stability is further increased by a definite but by no means excessive amount of understeer. This latest version of the DB2 is a car in which the driver feels particularly safe, the overall excellence of handling inspiring complete confidence even at very high speeds." *The Motor*'s summation was: "the DB2/4 can truthfully claim to be the fastest car in the world capable of carrying two people with a month's luggage". The only bad news was that the UK price had gone up by another £100, to £1850 basic (£2621 including purchase tax).

The DB2/4 would hold "two people with a month's luggage". The Bristol Freighter in the background will shortly be taking off for Le Touquet. Our friends seem to have missed this flight, as the aircraft's loading doors are closed.

Alongside the new saloon an equivalent drop-head coupé had been developed. Naturally it retained its normal boot lid, but otherwise it incorporated the same changes as the saloon, including the occasional seats at the rear. In order to accommodate the rear-seat passengers more comfortably, the hood was redesigned to increase its height in this area. Both a saloon (LML/518) and a drophead (unidentified, but possibly LML/558, registered 68 AMF) were on the Aston Martin stand at the 1953 Motor Show. The latter, which must have stood out in its ivory finish with red leather upholstery and red hood, was priced at £1950 basic (£2763 incl. PT), which meant that its price had also been increased by £100.

It was at about this time that the first of the special Bertone-bodied cars began to arrive in the United States. This was LML/504, a drophead coupé not designed by Bertone in-house but given to the freelance Giovanni Michelotti. It achieved some publicity, or one might say notoriety, in Britain as well as America, since it had been commissioned by 60 toadying district sales managers of a greetings card firm in Minneapolis, as a Christmas present to the firm's owner. It featured Michelotti's trademark heavy front grille plus extras such as a monogrammed steering-wheel, a cocktail cabinet and a bespoke leather ice-chest and picnic hamper. The remaining cars then arrived in drips and drabs – four over the first six months of 1954 and the two later chassis in 1955 and 1956. The bodies on these cars were all designed in-house by Bertone's chief stylist, Franco Scaglione. Apart from LML/765, which was a two-door fixed-head coupé, they were all open cars, either dropheads or "spiders" (sports). All are still in existence, excepting of course the mysterious LML/503 about which nothing is known.

In the spring of 1954 there appeared a road test in an obscure motoring magazine when *Top Gear* managed to borrow a car from the Scottish distributors (LML/616, registration LSC 920). The testers produced performance figures which were well ahead of what might have been expected, with a 0-60mph acceleration time of 10.9sec and a two-way average maximum speed of 114.6mph. One is

The drophead coupé shared most of the saloon's features but not, of course, the rear hatch. The drabness of early-1950s London emphasises the Aston Martin's glamour and style.

As with the saloon, the drophead coupé DB2/4 also gives access to the luggage compartment from the rear.

Door trim has become less complicated – no doubt in the pursuit of lower costs.

There is now a conventional external petrol filler.

almost inclined to believe that they had accidentally stumbled on a 2.9-litre car, but the factory records say otherwise, and one must instead suspect their timing methods. As to the car's handling, the testers found it "delightfully controllable". The weather had clearly not been kind to them, but they had not let this get in their way. "The car can be put into a four-wheel drift on wet or dry roads at 60, 80 or even over 100mph, and remain an utterly safe vehicle." Minor criticisms concerned the long clutch travel again, the seats ("perhaps a little austere and small for very long distance touring"), water entering at the rear door seals, and the jacking arrangements - they were unlucky enough to suffer a puncture. Overall, though, "the Aston Martin DB2/4 is a magnificent car offering the highest performance and roadability, yet has many practical features as an everyday motor-car".

Eventually the company had to come clean on the engine question, and it did so in late August

Note the one-piece windscreen – and the fact that this particular DB2/4 has lost its bumper overriders along the way.

Bumpers are now attached in a manner which protects the bodywork more effectively.

1954. "When the well-known DB2 Aston Martin engine was enlarged to 3 litres for competition purposes", gushed *The Motor*, "it seemed certain that an engine of this size would in due course be offered to the public. It is now history that in the first instance the Lagonda cars made by the same organization secured the advantage of this development, but for some time past the Aston Martins destined for America have had cylinder bores of 83mm rather than 78mm and have developed 140bhp in place of 125bhp. These modifications are now available to buyers on the home market." *The Autocar* were more cryptic in their news item, saying that the three-litre development (by which it was rapidly becoming known, rather than 2.9-litre) was "newly announced by the David Brown companies". The temptation to put through another price increase at the same time was too great for the company to resist. Basic prices for both saloon and drophead coupé went up by £75 to £1925 and £2025 respectively, bringing the totals

The bonnet has been raised in height compared with the DB2 to permit a greater installed height for the headlamps.

This car has the 2.9-litre engine, with triple horizontal twin-choke Weber carburettors.

including purchase tax to £2728 and 2869.

To accompany this news the company at last allowed the two journals to test a production version of the DB2/4. They were given the same car, LML/669 (4 AML), and it is instructive to compare their impressions. Who had the car first is impossible to say, but *The Motor* went as far as Belgium to do their testing, and as it happens they produced consistently better performance figures. Their standing-start times to 60 and 100mph were 10.5 and 30.0sec, compared with 11.1 and 31.7sec from *The Autocar*, and yet they claimed an overall fuel consumption of 23.0mpg against their rival's 20.1. These figures are in line with those obtained by Top Gear, and reflect the impact of the increased torque of the new engine being partially offset by the increase in weight. At least the two journals agreed on the car's top speed – 118mph – and its weight; at 24¾cwt (1257kg) this represents an increase over the DB2 of some 50kg.

The two reports are reassuringly similar in their

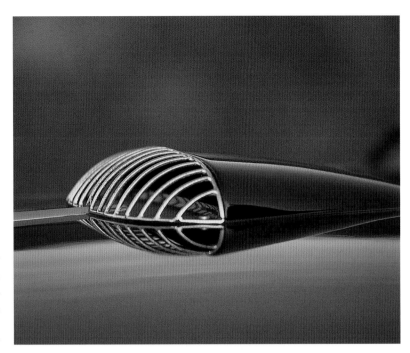

Some cars had this decorative grille over the scuttle air vent.

The one-piece opening bonnet gives superb access to both the engine and the front suspension.

main comments. Having praised yet again the car's unique combination of ride and roadholding, its "breathtaking" performance, its flexibility in top gear and the sweetness of its gearbox, they go on to point out how much wider will be the car's appeal now that it can accommodate two more passengers, even if only children can ride there in comfort for long. The luggage space is described as "ample" – indeed, if only two people are being carried and the backs of the rear seats are folded down, "the baggage space becomes almost unequalled in European cars". Both also praised the accessibility to the engine and front suspension afforded by the forward-opening bonnet assembly.

As against this praise, there were perhaps a few more criticisms than previously. The new petrol tank gave trouble, one magazine finding it difficult to fill without it blowing back and the other experiencing fuel starvation under acceleration when the level in the tank was low. Both disliked the long clutch travel, and both had reservations about the brakes, although one said there was pulling to one side during heavy braking and the other said there was not. The umbrella-type handbrake was not

liked, and a fly-off type was recommended to replace it. The interior driving mirror vibrated so much as to render it useless, and the cubbyholes each side of the instrument panel were too small and had no lip to retain their contents. Exhaust noise was close to being too loud, even for a sports car, and there were water leaks round both the doors and the new luggage-compartment lid. *The Motor* disliked the front seats, finding them lacking in both forward adjustment and lateral support; *The Autocar* found them "most comfortable".

It was probably a sign of the British motorist's growing maturity – and the disappearance of his "austerity" attitude of the immediate postwar years, when any new car was accepted gratefully – that minor criticisms like these were brought out into the open. The situation in North America was somewhat different in that there were no American models trying to satisfy the requirements of the more sporting minded, who had perforce to consider a "foreign" car. In that context the Aston Martin was one of a very few high-performance marques which carried a high price but was built to relatively luxurious standards, and the American

A DB2/4 (LML/693) privately entered by da Silva Ramos took part in the 1954 Le Mans race but retired. Here it is pursuing a Porsche.

buyer was usually impressed with what was offered for the price. This feeling comes out strongly in some road impressions of the DB2/4 published in the September 1954 issue of the American magazine *Road & Track* under the title "Family Sport Car".

The writer, Al Brannon, puts the "family" viewpoint right at the start: "If this baby won't satisfy anybody's requirements for a family bus with real sporting blood, they just aren't going to be satisfied". He continues with a loving description of the fittings and finish which make the car so special. Instruments, tool kit, boot light, adjustable steering-column all get singled out for praise, as does the general standard of finish. Even the seats, front and back, receive compliments, and the view to the front is likened to that from a Porsche – "You can almost see the ground going under the front bumper". Not that road behaviour is overlooked: "On bends the DB2/4 felt as though it was grabbing handfuls of the road, and when it did break loose it had a very flat four-wheel drift, with no dangerous tendencies apparent". No performance figures were taken during this road test

since the car was not yet fully run in.

When the time came for the London Show in 1954 the company made a point of highlighting the three-litre engine as a change introduced during the year, even though we now know that it was already under the bonnets of the previous year's exhibits. Once again there were examples of a saloon – LML/669 (4 AML), the *Motor* and *Autocar* road-test car – and a drophead coupé – LML/832 (NUK 555); this year they had to share stand space with the DB3S which had just gone on sale to the general public. By this time there were relatively few remaining British coachbuilders, but they still had their own section of the Show and demonstrated what they could build on the few separate chassis still on sale. It is a matter of some surprise that none of them chose to use the Aston Martin chassis, even though Bertone had shown what could be done with the nine chassis he had taken. Two other Turin coachbuilders built bodies on DB2/4 chassis, Allemano one and Vignale two.

Coachbuilding was still a sore point with the company management. Mulliners were making it increasingly obvious that the DB2/4's small volume

LML/669, the 1954 London Show car. It also featured in the 1956 motor racing film, Checkpoint, *starring Anthony Steel, Stanley Baker and James Robertson-Justice.*

*Success in the 1955
Monte Carlo Rally
justified an
advertising
campaign.*

just did not mix with the increasing number of Standard bodies which were going down the same line. This led to disagreements about both deliveries and price, to the benefit of neither side. The culmination was a decision to remove the work from Mulliners and place it instead with Tickford of Newport Pagnell in Buckinghamshire. The Tickford company – originally known as Salmons & Sons, a coachbuilding firm going back to 1820 – were in more recent times known as folding hood specialists. They had already been building the Lagonda drophead coupé and recently had gained the contract for the Lagonda saloon. Now they were to build both DB2/4 variants. It therefore made sense for the David Brown group to buy Tickford outright, and this is exactly what happened, at the very end of 1954. The press announcement made it clear that David Brown's objective was "to safeguard his automobile division against body-building difficulties such as have overtaken other makers of specialist cars".

By this time, it has recently been discovered, the David Brown Farsley works had taken over responsibility for final assembly. Although cars were still sent down to Feltham thereafter, it can only have been for their final pre-delivery check. Just how long the Farsley production line had been in operation is unclear, but it is not impossible that it began eighteen months previously as a response to the DB2/4's early production problems. With the acquisition of the Tickford facility, however, it was logical to move assembly there as well, and Newport Pagnell came to take centre stage in the affairs of David Brown's Automobile Division.

Meanwhile, the company continued to pursue an aggressive programme of competitive events. Although the spotlight continued to fall on the flagship, the DB3S, there were still outings available for the bread-and-butter model from time to time. One such opportunity was the 1955 Monte Carlo Rally, for which three works entries were prepared, LML/784, /855 and /857 (55, 56 and 54 DMF); drivers were Gatsonides/Becquart, Parnell/Klementaski and Collins/Whitehead. They finished respectably: the Gatsonides' team were first in their class and seventh overall, while the Collins and Parnell cars were eleventh and seventeenth respectively in the class. At one point Gatsonides and Becquart seemed to be heading for victory, until a secret check caught them out. Later, at the Concours d'Elegance, the Gatsonides/Becquart car won the RAC Trophy for Comfort and Road Safety, and the three cars' high

The previously unknown assembly line for DB2/4s at the David Brown Farsley works.

standard of equipment and turn-out won them a newly-created team prize. Their list of equipment shows how much preparation had gone into the cars: twin chronometers on the dashboard, matt painted; an extra windscreen-wiper, high-mounted and vacuum-operated; electric demisters; a spare dipswitch, and more. Then came the navigator's equipment, including a map table, map box, torch, camera and duplicate horn button. Also in the car's interior were thermos flasks, cans of self-heating soup and a crowbar. Once you reached the luggage boot it started all over again – tow rope, snow mats, snow chains, petrol, oil and a second spare wheel. Under the bonnet were spare plugs, a spare coil and a spare starter solenoid.

Two cars, 54 DMF and 56 DMF, were then entered in that year's Mille Miglia, to be driven by Tommy Wisdom and Paul Frere respectively, but both retired early on through clutch failure (Borg & Beck were blamed for supplying the wrong clutch). A DB3S was also entered for Collins, but he suffered a blown engine. This was the year when Moss won with a Mercedes-Benz 300SLR at an average speed of nearly 100mph, so there was little hope of glory for the Aston Martins even if they had held together. As Wyer saw it, their one and only chance of winning this race had been the year before.

At this period the DB2/4 looked reasonably competitive, at least on the British market. There were very few British-made cars in the same price range; the Three-litre Alvis and the Bristol 405 come to mind, at £2300 and £2390 (basic) respectively, compared with the DB2/4 saloon at £2050, but they offered nowhere near the same performance. Of course there was the Jaguar XK140 fixed-head coupé which could reach 60mph in 11 seconds, had a maximum speed of 129mph and cost only £1140; no-one seemed able to approach

The Bristol 405 was in the same price bracket as the DB2/4 but could not compete on performance.

Jaguar's value-for-money. Foreign cars in those days were penalised by heavy import duties, so it is not surprising that the BMW 507, for example, which was good for 135mph, was priced at a heady £2800. The Mercedes-Benz 300SL cost even more – £3100 – but it would eat the DB2/4 for breakfast with its 140mph top speed and acceleration from rest to 60mph in less than nine seconds. The Aston Martin's advantage, apart from price, over all these models was that it could offer four seats of a sort. The Porsche 356A Carrera was competitive on performance and price, at £1910, but again it could only offer two seats. In overseas markets, of course, such as the United States, these price differentials were somewhat reduced. Nevertheless the DB2/4's price – even though it was now approaching $7000 – coupled with its 2+2 seating, still made it competitive with its main rivals.

The Jaguar XK140 fixed-head coupé offered a similar kind of car to the Aston Martin, and at a significantly lower price.

During the course of the summer plans were finalised to move production – that is, the assembly of the body to the chassis – from Farsley to Newport Pagnell. This coincided with a series of minor changes to the body design, which collectively justified a new model name: DB2/4 Mark II. When production of the DB2/4 ceased, some 565 cars had emerged from Feltham over a period of two years, a creditable record for a small firm using hand-built methods, and a figure which would not be surpassed until the arrival of the DB5. There were organisational changes, too: importantly, the technical and organisational talents which John Wyer had brought to his duties as chief development engineer were recognised and he was promoted to the Aston Martin board with the title of Technical Director; the following year David Brown appointed him General Manager of the company. Harold Beach, Chief Engineer under Wyer, said years later, "I regarded John Wyer's appointment as the most significant development in the Aston Martin story, for a true sense of direction and purpose descended on Feltham".

Another rival to the DB2/4 was the Mercedes-Benz 300SL which, with 215bhp, offered much superior performance to the DB2/4 though only two seats. UK import duties made it very expensive, however. This example is seen on the 1959 Monte Carlo Rally.

Harold Beach, Chief Engineer under John Wyer.

DB2/4 – Summary Statistics

Engine

configuration	6 cylinders in line, overhead valves, twin overhead camshafts
capacity	2580/2922cc
bore	78/83mm
stroke	90mm
RAC rating	22.6/25.6hp
compression ratio	8.16:1
firing order	153624
valve timing	io 18° atdc,
tappet clearances (cold)	.inlet .014-.016in, exhaust .017-.019in
brake horsepower	125/140 @ 5000rpm
crankshaft	
no of bearings	4
main bearing	2½in (63.5mm) diameter
big end	2ins (51mm diameter)
crankcase capacity	15 pints (8.5 litres)
cooling system	water pump, thermostat bypass, capacity 3 galls (13.6 litres)
ignition details	Lucas, coil, 12 volts
ignition timing	5° btdc
contact breaker gap	.012in
plugs – make/gap	KLG P10 L80 10mm/.022in
carburettors	Twin 1¾in SU HV6
fuel pump	Twin SU electric
clutch	Borg & Beck single plate type 9A6G
engine number location	Front of timing cover AND on bulkhead plate

Gearbox

type	David Brown 4-speed
gear ratios	3.73, 4.96, 7.38 and 10.9 to 1; reverse 10.9:1
oil capacity	2¼ pints (1.3 litres)

Chassis

wheelbase	99in (2515mm)
track	54in (1372mm)
length	169½in (4305mm)
width	65in (1651mm)
weight (dry)	2600lb (1179kg)
turning circle	35ft (10.7m)
suspension	independent at front, live axle at rear, coil springs all round
wheels and tyres	Dunlop centre-lock wires, 6.00 x 16in
tyre pressures	26psi front, 27psi rear (30/31psi for high speed driving)
brakes	Girling 2LS hydraulic, drums 12in diameter
steering box	Marles worm and double roller
propeller shaft	Open, Hardy Spicer
rear axle	hypoid bevel, Salisbury
ratio	3.73:1
oil capacity	2½ pints (1.4 litres)
shock absorbers	Armstrong - DAS 10R (front), DAS 12R (rear)
petrol tank capacity	17 galls (77 litres), incl 3 galls (14 litres) reserve
chassis number location	Offside front of frame AND on bulkhead plate

Prices (excl. purchase tax)

saloon	1953: £1850, 1954: £1925
drophead coupé	1953: £1950, 1954: £2025

Numbers Produced

saloon	451
drophead coupé	102
other	12
Total	565

Chapter Six

The DB2/4
Marks II & III

The changes brought about in the Mark II are almost entirely confined to the body, and the catalyst, once again, was the need to hold down costs. At the same time the company made a serious effort to respond to such criticisms as had been made about the DB2/4. Thus the height of the saloon's roof is raised by three-quarters of an inch (19mm), but to avoid specifying a new windscreen (and thus have different screens for saloon and drophead) the gap is filled by a chromium "bandage" above the screen. The expensive aluminium casting for the sill and door hinge-post is deleted, and the bonnet/wings assembly is simplified and lightened by arranging that the side panels behind the front wheel arches remain fixed. This makes no difference to engine accessibility, and at the same time allows small ventilator panels to be added in this area, which

A DB2/4 Mk II saloon in an unusual two-tone finish. Note the Tickford badge on the bonnet side, and the chrome "bandage" over the windscreen.

The increased roof height of the Mk II is very evident in this shot.

We have already met this car in the previous chapter, in colour. Although really a Mk I, it was modified to look like a Mark II and used in company publicity shots.

can direct cool air to the footwells. The semaphore indicators formerly in this position are deleted in favour of the new-style flashing indicators. This leaves a visible join between bonnet and wing which is disguised by a chromium strip, with a Tickford badge below it. At the rear the wing line is raised to form a small fin in the fashion of the times, and the rear lights are raised in height accordingly. The petrol filler reverts to being concealed under a flap, which can only be opened from inside the car.

Inside there are further changes. The British journalists' dislike of an umbrella-type handbrake has seen to it that it is replaced by a true diehard's fly-off type. The seats are given more lateral support, and of course the increase in roof height translates into a welcome improvement in head-room, particularly over the rear seats. There are now courtesy switches to operate the roof lights. As for the engine, although the 140bhp version of the three-litre was the standard offering, it was possible to specify a special series version (VB6J/.../L) which had larger valves and higher-lift camshafts, and which was stated to produce 165bhp. Numerous further extras were available for competition purposes, such as higher-compression pistons, a twin exhaust system, integral oil-cooler, a close-ratio gearbox, Alfin brake drums and 40 DCO Weber carburettors. The only change to the transmission was the fitting of an uprated rear axle, of Salisbury manufacture once again, to handle the higher engine output.

The new model was introduced at the 1955 London Motor Show, but the two familiar body styles, saloon and drophead coupe, were accompanied by a third, a fixed-head coupé. This latest design could be traced back to a works prototype DB2/4, chassis LML/515, which started life as a drophead coupé in 1953 but was then sent to Mulliners for conversion. The brief – to add a "hard top" in the same shape as the drophead's hood – was judged to have been very well executed, and the attractive notchback design was introduced as part of the Mk II launch. Known either as the "hardtop" or the "fixed head coupé", its upper part was often finished in a contrasting colour. It was priced at the same level as the saloon, and inevitably the launch of the Mk II was accompanied by another price increase. The saloon and hardtop were now £2050 basic, £2905 including purchase tax, while the figures for the drophead coupé were £2200 and £3117.

During 1956 the company began a connection

Rear view of a Mk II saloon, showing the vestigial fins and the flap concealing the petrol filler. The new bonnet arrangement, with the side panels remaining fixed, is also visible.

with a new Italian coachbuilder, Touring, who built a run of three "Spyder" (two-seater) designs on chassis AM300/1161-3. Aston Martin intended to standardise this as an export-only model. The particular interest in these cars was that they used Touring's patented "Superleggera" (super-light)

Interior of a fixed-head coupé. The central fly-off handbrake can just be seen.

The prototype fixed-head coupé. This started life as a Mk I drophead coupé (chassis LML/515) and was modified by Mulliners – hence no Tickford badge.

A Mark II, chassis AM/300/1161 was bodied by Touring of Milan. This car was the prize in a national newspaper competition.

system of multiple small-diameter tubes, on which the light-alloy bodywork panels rested but were not rigidly fixed. This connection with the Milan company was of course to have important consequences for the future direction of Aston Martin, starting with the DB4 model. Mechanically the car was a standard DB2/4 Mk II except for the engine, which used the uprated cylinder head (an optional extra on the home market) with larger inlet and exhaust valves and high-lift cams, coupled with the dual exhaust system, which raised the power from 140bhp at 5000rpm to 165bhp at 5500rpm.

The three Spyders were used to gain maximum publicity during the autumn of 1956. One (/1162)

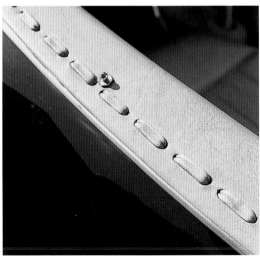

went to the Paris Show, another (/1163) was on the Aston Martin stand at the Earls Court Show, and the third was purchased by *The Daily Mail* and offered as a prize in connection with the Show. The prize was won by an apprentice joiner from Scotland after his tie-break slogan, "Who said a Spyder can't fly?" was judged the best. With it came the car and £700 – a good sum of money in those days – for running expenses. The winner did not hold a driving licence, and at that time of the Suez fuel crisis could not take a driving test even if he wanted to. On the other hand he could, under the temporary regulations then in force, have held a provisional licence for one month and then driven the (left-hand drive) car legally – until his monthly fuel ration of 10½ gallons (48 litres) was used up.

This "Spyder" design is only a two-seater.

Interior trim is of a high standard, as shown by this decorative stitching.

Touring's badge was prominent on the bonnet and at the rear, but unlike with the Arnolt cars the manufacturer's name was not in doubt.

Superleggera (super-light) was Touring's patent system of body construction using multiple small-diameter tubes.

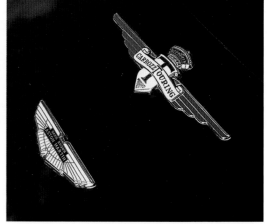

Just prior to the London Show an extraordinary announcement had appeared in the motoring press. "David Brown to specialise," ran the head-line, "At the beginning of this week all models of the Aston Martin and Lagonda, except for the stan-dard saloon version, ceased production. The saloon prices remain unchanged. An exception to

*Characteristic
chrome treatment
round the rear
window of the Mark
II saloon. The trim
continues from
above the
windscreen along the
top of the side
windows and rejoins
the waist flash.*

the above will be a new export Aston Martin to be seen for the first time at the Paris Show. It will have a two-seater open body designed and built by Carrozzeria Touring of Milan, and will be called the Superleggera. The basic price of this car will be £2,500." The immediate consequence seemed to be that only a saloon, and no drophead or fixed-head coupé, appeared on the company stand at Earls Court alongside the Touring Spyder. Yet the other two models continued to appear in the price lists, and indeed the "hardtop" (fixed-head) – although not the drophead – figured specifically in a price-cut announcement some five months later. Moreover the two coupé models continued in production, although admittedly this could have been against orders already received. The announcement also seems to have marked the end of the DB3S model being made available to the general public.

The price cut referred to was announced in March 1957, and involved a £125 reduction in the basic price of both the saloon and the hardtop. This brought the total price after purchase tax for both models to £2888. The announcement went on to say, "Sales efforts made in the Western Hemisphere to counteract the effect of reduced sales resulting from petrol rationing have led to an unbalanced demand for left hand drive models. This price reduction is calculated to bring the demand for rhd models into line". Decoding this early example of corporate gobbledegook, one might deduce that the company had too many right hand drive chassis in stock. Coupled with the earlier announcement about specialising in a single model, it seems clear that more generally there was a severe sales problem – probably common to all manufacturers of larger-engined cars at that time of fuel shortage, although the Mark II saloon's somewhat top-heavy appearance may also have been a factor. Underlying the company's concerns was the need to clear Mark II stocks ready for the launch of the Mark III, and in taking these decisions one can perhaps detect the hand of John Wyer who at about this time was promoted to the position of General Manager of the Automotive Division.

By now the various versions of the DB2 and DB2/4 were relatively familiar sights on British roads, and were well known to enthusiasts round the world. It is hardly surprising that evolutionary changes to the model were less newsworthy than they had been in the past – and certainly less newsworthy than the more glamorous competition models, the DB3 and its successors the DB3S and DBR series. Thus there had been no apparent clamour from the journalistic fraternity to borrow examples of the Mk II for road testing, and it was not until the spring of 1957 that any such test appeared. This was in *Autosport*, whose contrib-

At first glance the Mark II DB2/4 saloon is little changed. This is chassis AM300/1159.

utor John Bolster tested a standard 140bhp saloon (AM300/1145, 4 JHX) in May of that year.

Since his last test in 1951, the car's engine size had gone up from 2.6 to three litres, and it had grown two more seats and considerably more luggage space. On that last point Bolster commented that "the luggage platform is actually larger than that of some small station wagons". He also appreciated the improvements which had been made to both the clutch and the brakes; his remark that they would stand much more punishment than before suggests that both were known to be weak areas. The brakes "are capable of arresting the car repeatedly from high speeds

New rear lights are mounted on slightly more protruding wings.

The Tickford badge is mounted on the side panel, just above the new opening ventilator.

This shot shows the new bonnet arrangement, whereby the side panels remain fixed.

The Tickford badge and side ventilator panels are other recognition points.

This rear view shows clearly the increased overall height.

The saloon's rear door gives a truly cavernous opening. Luggage space is more than adequate, and can be increased by folding down the back of the rear seat.

without fading, and only by an occasional slight whistle do they show that a lot is being asked of them". Another much welcomed change was the move to a fly-off handbrake instead of the previous umbrella type. A single criticism was that there was insufficient clearance round his right foot on the accelerator pedal.

As to performance on the road, Bolster achieved a 0-60mph acceleration time of 9.8 seconds, which was the fastest time so far from any DB2 series car, and a top speed of 118.4mph in less than perfect conditions. His assessment of the car's roadholding was typical of the man: "Much of the reputation of the DB2-4 comes from its capacity to recover after the driver has been over-enterprising. This stems largely from the exceptionally 'quick' steering,

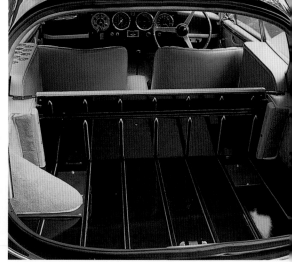

Two views of DB2/4 Mk II chassis AM300/1202 - one of the last Mark IIs.

which is ideal for catching a skid before it has developed". The gearbox was "one of the easiest to handle that has ever been made". Overall, his summary was that the DB2-4 Mk II was "a very sporting car that you can drive in a dinner jacket".

At about the same period Roy Salvadori, a well-known competition driver and member of the Aston Martin works team, carried out a road test of the same car for *Autocourse and Sporting Motorist* magazine. Although there were few startling insights, the overall tone was reassuring, and in particular he approved of the brakes and the lighter pedal pressure now needed. Even now, however, he still complained about the long clutch travel required for full disengagement. His performance figures were very similar to those from Bolster's *Autosport* test: 0-60mph in 10.0

Above: The rear compartment is light and airy.

seconds and a maximum speed of 119.2mph. Overlapping these two assessments of the Mark II model came the first announcement of its successor, the Mark III. Featured first at the Geneva Show in March 1957, and launched simultaneously in the United States, it was stated to be for export only – not a difficult feat, since some 80% of production was already being exported – but this

Right: The large handle which releases the forward-opening bonnet can be seen below the instrument panel.

Far Right: The Mark II was given a fly-off handbrake in place of the previous umbrella type.

A company publicity shot of the DB2/4 Mk III – clearly a prototype since it still uses the "refrigerator" door handle.

was only a cover story while stocks of the Mark II in the home market were run down. The Mark II had not been a sales disaster, but it had suffered from the plunge in demand during the Suez crisis, and as a result only sold 199 examples in its two-year life from October 1955 to October 1957. This contrasted poorly with its predecessor, the DB2/4, which in a corresponding period (1953-1955) sold 565 cars, or nearly three times the rate of sale. During the time the Mark II was on sale it became obvious to the company that the model's performance had to be improved if it was to keep up with its competitors, and that the answer was to transfer some of the engine technology which had been so expensively acquired in developing the DB3S.

Eberan von Eberhorst had returned to Auto Union Germany in 1953 (and eventually became a lecturer at the Technical Institute of Vienna). His place was taken by an engineer of Polish origin, Tadek Marek, who joined Aston Martin from Austin and remained with them until his retirement. Marek was put to work on a new block for the three-litre engine – a matter of urgency if only because the original patterns were wearing out. He

sought above all else to overcome the inherent weaknesses in a barrel-type block/crankcase structure, probably bearing in mind the infamous barb from Alec Issigonis, "with a barrel crankcase the shaft supports the case, not vice versa!" In what amounted to a total redesign of the engine, using the company's racing experience wherever appropriate, Marek's solution was to stiffen both the crankcase, by adding extra webs, and the crankshaft by use of improved materials and hardening methods. The crankshaft was also made more resistant to failure by the all-important addition of larger fillet radii at the junctions between journals and webs.

A further radical change to the original design was in the means of sealing the wet liners. Up to this point they had always been "bottom-seating", originally using Hallite wire-reinforced figure-of-eight washers and then changing to copper. The top seal was of course the cylinder head gasket, and great care was needed during assembly to equalise the amount of "nip" on the liner when the head was pulled down, involving both careful selection of gasket thickness and even lapping in

DB2/4 Mk III fixed-head coupe, chassis AM/300/3/1830, one of the last Mark IIIs.

The frontal appearance of the Mk III is changed significantly compared with its predecessors.

the individual liners. Experience eventually showed that each liner should project between .002 and .003in above the block, and that there should be no more than .0005in difference between adjacent liners. The compression which this induced in the liner often made them distort under conditions of high thermal loading, leading to a blown head-gasket. Marek changed the system to "top-seating", with pairs of O-rings providing the seal at the bottom. There are bleed holes between the pairs of rings to provide an escape route for any coolant which might have leaked in under pressure, and the factory personnel found they could use these holes to pressure-test the liners during engine assembly.

These changes to the bottom end of the engine gave Marek the confidence to increase the power output through improvements at its top end. There

The elegant lines of the fixed-head coupé are apparent in this side view.
Like the Mark II, Mark III models bear the Tickford badge on their bonnet sides.

The fixed-head's appearance is enhanced by the two-tone paint treatment.

The rear lights are slimmer and more elegant than those on the Mark II.

Rear number-plate treatment on the fixed-head coupé is particularly neat.

are revisions to the cylinder-head and manifolds, which again show lessons learned from racing experience. Inlet valves are increased in diameter from 1.50in (38mm) to 1.675ins (42.5mm), valve seat inserts are deleted, rubber seals are fitted in the valve guides, spark plugs are now 14mm instead of 10mm, porting is improved, camshafts on both inlet and exhaust sides give higher lift, and there is a new inlet manifold to suit the twin 1½in

The coupé's boot capacity is substantial for a car of the period. There is a recess for tools at the rear edge of the boot.

This particular car has the optional twin exhaust system.

This car has the DBD-series engine with triple SU carburettors.

SU H6 carburettors now being fitted. The chain drive to the water pump is scrapped, the pump now being belt driven. The tensioners for the two timing chains are now manually adjusted, replacing the previous automatic hydraulic adjusters which had been a source of problems. A completely new type of oil-pump is driven through a worm and wheel instead of the previous spiral gears, which had been inclined to wear too

quickly. The flywheel has been lightened, and for the first time the clutch is of the hydraulic self-adjusting type.

The engine in the specification described above is known as the DBA series, and was stated at the time to produce 162bhp. With a twin exhaust system fitted, however, the output apparently goes up to 178bhp. Other mechanical changes concern the brakes, where Alfin brake drums are now stan-

As before, side panels remain fixed when the bonnet is opened.

Chassis AM300/3/ 1387. The re-shaped bonnet to suit the new grille is very evident.

dardised. However, it was possible to specify disc brakes at the front at extra cost. As for external changes, the most obvious is a new grille, a Frank Feeley design clearly based on that of the DB3S and destined to influence the appearance of Aston Martins for many years to come. The bonnet is lowered and reshaped to suit the new grille. The

frontal appearance is also improved by the deletion of the Mk II's chrome "bandage" above the windscreen. Through ventilation is assisted by the provision of opening rear quarter-lights, hinged at their forward edges. The layout of the instrument panel is entirely new, with the main dials grouped around the steering column directly in front of the

Chassis AM300/3/ 1605. The lack of chrome trim above the wind-screen and side windows shows up clearly.

driver; again, this principle would be followed on many future models. A new style of door handle replaced the former design, which had remained unchanged since the very first DB2 and which is said to have been originally manufactured for a refrigerator. At the rear, the Mark II's somewhat pimply tail lamps are replaced by a taller, more elegant design.

Nothing was said about price at the time of the Geneva and New York launches, other than a reference in one journal to "about $6950" for a "standard" version. However, at the London launch in October 1957 the UK prices were announced, and they turned out (for the saloon) to be exactly those in force for the Mark II until its price cut

This car, AM300/3/ 1610, was the subject of a road-test in Country Life *in November 1958.*

An early left-hand drive Mk III, AM300/3/1316, originally exported to Sweden, showing the revised tail and rear-lamp treatment. The new instrument panel is just visible.

The Mark III's new style of door-handle, mounted higher up, is clear on this shot of chassis AM300/3/1531.

earlier in the year. In other words the price reduction had all along been intended as a short-term measure to clear the last Mk II stocks. Thus the new prices were for the saloon £2050 basic and £3076 with tax, and for the drophead coupé £2300 basic and £3451 with tax. It will be noted that the differential between the two models had increased from £150 to £250, and that there was still no fixed-head coupé. Examples of both models were on the company stand at Earls Court, the saloon in desert white and the drophead in satin bronze.

At the same time there were two announcements concerning changes in specification. Firstly, the previously optional front disc brakes were now standardised; in fact it was only the first 100 chassis, known internally as Mark IIIAs, which did not have discs; thereafter, from chassis /1401, the specification was known as the Mark IIIB. Secondly, it became possible to specify that peculiarly British extra, the Laycock-de Normanville overdrive unit, which bolted on to the back of the gearbox and operated on top gear only. All this publicity clearly had an effect, since at the end of the Show the company were able to announce that they had sold out their total 1958 allocation, both

home and export; they stated that the export allocation had been taken up mainly in North America, France and Belgium.

It was not until December that a motoring journal was allowed to try out the Mark III. *The Autocar*, as was becoming normal for fast cars, took it to the Continent for performance testing, at which it performed quite impressively. Their first reaction was, "The car represents a considerable improvement over the previous model, even though the increase in power does only a little more than offset an addition of nearly 1½cwt [76kg] to an already heavy design". Their particular car, AM300/3B/1401 (147 MMC), was fitted with overdrive, and the top speed figures which it produced were almost identical to those on normal top – 118mph against 119. Acceleration times recorded were 0-60mph in 9.3 seconds (a new benchmark) and 0-100mph in 31.0 seconds. Thus there was no perceptible gain in maximum speed compared with the old model, although the journalists made the point that if the dual-exhaust model with its extra 16bhp were specified, then there were plenty of rpm in hand on overdrive to permit a higher maximum.

They made special mention of the benefit of

using overdrive on the much-envied Continental roads: "It made cruising between 80 and 100mph restful, almost to the point of seeming a leisurely form of travel". The assessment was that using the overdrive for medium-speed cruising brought both a significant reduction in exhaust noise and gains in fuel economy; they achieved 18.1mpg overall for their Continental tour, and estimated the normal range to be 16-22mpg. There was high praise, too, for the new instrument panel, its new location directly in front of the driver meriting the description "splendid", and the power of the head-lamps was at last enough to satisfy the testers. On the other hand there were plenty of minor criticisms: the spring-loading on the gear selector mechanism – different on the overdrive model – made gear-changing awkward, there were two noticeable vibration periods in the engine, the tyres lost grip in the wet, the disc brakes did not bring as great an improvement as had been expected, the horns were weak and the heater output could be greater. (The comment about the tyres caused some controversy and led to the Avon tyre company arranging some back-to-back tests which were reported later in the same magazine.) Nevertheless the testers' conclusion was still that "a successful attempt has been made to combine the exhilaration of high-speed travel with the luxury of refined transport".

Since the acquisition of Tickfords at the end of 1954, there had been a steady transfer of production processes from the David Brown factory at Farsley near Leeds, and final inspection at Feltham, to the Tickford works at Newport Pagnell. At the beginning of 1958 *The Autocar* were invited to visit the Tickford works to see how much progress had been achieved, and it was impressive. Although it had not proved necessary to add any more buildings to the site, there had clearly been a major investment programme in machine tools and other equipment. Virtually all machining of engine components, and their subsequent assembly and testing, now took place there. The only exceptions were the crankshafts, which arrived as a complete balanced assembly including flywheel and clutch, and the gearbox and clutch-housing assembly which was made as a unit at the David Brown gearbox factory at Huddersfield. Chassis were now also made from scratch at Newport Pagnell.

The bodies of course continued to be made there as well. This involved building up by spot- and arc-welding a frame of steel strip and tube to form a complete structure which could then be

ASTON MARTIN
1959 DB MARK III MODELS

standard and special series

The ASTON MARTIN DB MARK III saloon and drophead coupe 1959 models are now available in standard and special series versions. There are now five ASTON MARTIN models from which you may choose. See your nearest dealer today, or write direct to ASTON MARTIN LAGONDA LIMITED, Hanworth Park, Feltham, Middlesex.

The Special Series specification includes three carburetters, 8.6:1 compression ratio with a twin exhaust system.

ASTON MARTIN DB MARK III

Standard Saloon £2,050 or £3,076 7s inc. P. Tax

Special Series Saloon £2,120 or £3,181 7s inc. P. Tax

Standard Drophead Coupe (as illustrated) £2,300 or £3,451 7s inc. P. Tax

Special Series Drophead Coupe £2,370 or £3,556 7s inc. P. Tax

Aston Martin DB4 £2,650 or £3,976 7s inc. P. Tax

Aston Martin Lagonda Ltd A David Brown Company · Hanworth Park Feltham Middlesex

London Showrooms: 96/97 Piccadilly London W1 *Telephone:* GROsvenor 7747

London Distributors: Brooklands of Bond Street Ltd W1 *Telephone:* GROsvenor 8351

clad in aluminium. This frame was then taped and graphite-greased before the panels, in 16-gauge except for the bonnet which is 14-gauge, were attached and welded together. The whole structure was then assembled to the chassis by a series of 5/16in bolts and tack-welding. There had been some further weight reduction in the intervening time, as the boot lid was now aluminium instead of steel, its large window was 3/16in glass instead of ¼in, and both the rear seat pan and the gearbox cover were moulded in glass fibre.

During 1958 some further engine modifications began to trickle down from the racing programme. As well as the standard DBA engine, and the optional twin exhaust system, a DBB series was announced which had triple carburettors – either Weber 35 DCO twin-choke or SU HV6 – coupled

Advertising for the Mark III in late 1958 highlighted the Special Series engine with triple SU carburettors, an 8.6:1 compression ratio, modified camshafts and a twin exhaust system, producing 195bhp as against the standard engine's 162bhp.

with a higher (8.6:1) compression ratio and modified camshafts. Including the twin exhaust system, which was standard with this configuration, the DBB option cost an extra £70 basic, and together the changes produced 195bhp; DBB engines were fitted to only 10 cars. Later in the year, at the time of the London Show, an intermediate configuration known as the DBD series was announced, which was otherwise similar to the DBB but had the triple SU carburettors. Output for this specification was quoted as 180bhp and this engine was fitted to 47 chassis. There is also thought to have been a DBC version which used 45 DCO Weber carburettors and delivered 214bhp, but it was apparently only fitted to one car.

That year's Show, of course, saw the introduction of the new DB4 model, and understandably the spotlight swung away from the DB2/4. The main story to be told about the latter concerned

the engine options described above, and the only other change introduced was the addition of a Baldwin hydraulic booster in the braking system, said to improve brake effectiveness at lower pedal pressures. The cars on the stand were once again a drophead coupé (probably AM300/3/1490, 110 RMA) and a saloon. Prices were unchanged from the previous year, at £2050 basic (£3076 with tax) for the saloon and £2300 (£3451) for the drophead.

There followed two further road tests of the Mark III, in quick succession. In December 1958 *Road & Track* put a standard DBA-engined single-exhaust (162bhp) model through its paces, and were full of praise for virtually everything except its "astronomical" price (quoted at $7450). Picked out for particular compliments was the road-holding – understandably since the typical American product still offered a "boulevard ride" which was only acceptable in a straight line. "The

On the Mark III the instruments are grouped directly in front of the driver.

The Jaguar XK150 provided strong competition for the Mark III, particularly because of its price. It came with 3.4- and 3.8-litre engines giving outputs ranging from 190 to 265bhp.

fun increases in direct proportion to the pace ... the car does handle superbly ... it has to be felt to be believed." Steering, gearbox, instruments and general comfort were all applauded. As to performance, the testers reached a two-way average top speed of 118mph and an acceleration time from rest to 60mph of just over 9 seconds, virtually identical figures to those produced by *The Autocar* a year earlier in a similarly-powered car.

A month later Aston Martin works driver Roy Salvadori managed to trump all previous road tests by getting his hands on a DBB-engined car on behalf of *Autocourse and Sporting Motorist*. This was AM300/3/1408 (98 MMG), fitted with over-drive in conjunction with the optional lower rear axle ratio of 4.09:1. Needless to say he set up an all-time record for these tests with a 0-60mph time of 8.2 seconds, but to do this he decided, on his own admission, to use something like 6000rpm rather than the manufacturer's recommended

maximum of 5500. He also achieved an accelera-tion time from rest to 100mph of 23.8 seconds, a three-second improvement over his previous performance in a Mark II. His comments in two areas – roadholding in the wet, and brakes – are especially interesting, since they directly contradict *The Autocar*'s criticisms the previous year. Salvadori goes out of his way to compliment the Avon Turbospeeds for their wet-weather handling, and one can only conclude that Avon and Aston Martin between them had worked hard on the problem in the intervening time. His only major negative comment is reserved, yet again, for the exhaust system; here, with his inside knowledge, he lets the cat out of the bag by revealing that "a more prudish silencing system would impair the extra power provided by three carburettors". In summary, he felt that "the gradual elimination of small faults over the years has resulted in a sports car that fulfils its purpose to perfection".

One last upgrade in specification to the Mark III was announced in early-1959 – the availability of Borg Warner automatic transmission, at an additional basic price of £150. Possibly no other change over the life of the various DB2 models better sums up the car's journey from hard-nosed sports car to luxurious businessman's express. The company claimed not only that there was there no fall-off in performance but also that acceleration up to 60mph was actually improved. This presumably took account of the fact that most owners with manual gearboxes would change up from second to third before reaching this speed, rather than continuing into territory only explored by Roy Salvadori.

In spite of the publicity surrounding the DB4, the Mark III continued in production alongside the new model for another nine months, until July 1959. It could not have done so without maintaining its competitiveness, both in Britain and worldwide, and a comparison with its immediate opposition at this date is instructive. Amongst British makes of the period Jaguar were still offering outstanding value-for-money, and made the Mark III look expensive. By this time the XK150 was on the market, and like the Mark III it had two occasional seats at the back. Its performance, with acceleration to 60mph in 8.5 seconds and a maximum of 124mph, was comparable, but the price was not – only £1175 basic against the Mark III's £2050. Jaguar apart, however, there were not many others to choose from. The Jensen 541R was possibly the closest, priced at £1910 basic (£2866 with purchase tax) and no slouch in performance terms with its 123mph top speed and a 0-100mph time just over 30 seconds. On the other hand it lacked the tradition and competition record which were associated with the Aston Martin name. Other British cars in the price bracket were the Three-Litre Alvis (£1995 basic) and the more expensive Bristol 406 (£2995), but these were

The 1953 Jensen 541, which had a 4-litre six-cylinder ohv engine. In later 150bhp 541R form it was a close rival for the Mark III Aston, capable of 0-100mph in just over 30 seconds and a top speed of 123mph.

The Alfa Romeo 1900 Super Sprint matched the Mark III Aston Martin in price but not in seating capacity. The engine was a sparkling Alfa four-cylinder dohc unit, but the gearchange was on the column.

Import duties made the glamorous 3.2-litre BMW 507 much more expensive than the Mark III on the British market.

significantly slower and appealed to a more conservative type of owner. And of course there was now another very comparable car against which the Mark III's price had been made deliberately attractive: the DB4, at £2650.

On the other hand imported makes were becoming a more common sight on British roads, in spite of the import duties imposed on them. The much-admired Lancia Aurelia GT, for example, with a basic price of £2330, was another car with 2+2 seating and a reasonably competitive maximum speed (110mph). There were also a couple of two-seaters – Alfa-Romeo Super Sprint (£2250) and Porsche 356A Carrera (£2220) – at similar prices to the Mark III. Thereafter prices moved rapidly into the stratosphere, through the BMW 507 (£3100) to the Mercedes 300SL roadster (£3750) and Ferrari 250GT (£4200, or £6469 with purchase tax), all these latter cars being two-

seaters. In overseas markets, of course, particularly the United States, the Continental makes were at less of a disadvantage. Nevertheless the Mark III, even priced at more than $7000, was an attractive proposition, particularly with its four-seat configuration.

So the Mark III allowed the DB2 range to go out with a bang. In the two years and four months it had been in production it had sold no less than 551 examples – almost as many as the Mark I DB2/4, and more than either the Mark II DB2/4 or the original DB2. Its appeal to overseas and particularly American buyers was maintained to the end, with nearly two thirds of all production going to the United States. Although its sporting achievements were overshadowed by those of the DB3 and DB3S, it laid the foundation of those later successes, and its engineering principles formed a solid foundation for the design of the later cars.

Amongst imported cars the Lancia Aurelia GT was much admired, with a performance not far short of the Mark III's from its 2.5-litre V6 engine. Here Villoresi is flagged off on the 1957 Acropolis Rally, which he won.

Summary Statistics

	DB2/4 Mark II	**DB Mk III**
Engine		
configuration	6 cylinders in line, overhead valves, twin overhead camshafts	6 cylinders in line, overhead valves, twin overhead camshafts
capacity	2922cc	2922cc
bore	83mm	83mm
stroke	90mm	90mm
RAC rating	25.6hp	25.6hp
compression ratio	8.16:1	8.16:1
firing order	153624	153624
valve timing	io 18° atdc	io 18° atdc
tappet clearances (cold)	.inlet .014-.016in, exhaust .017-.019in	.inlet .014-.016in, exhaust .017-.019in
brake horsepower	140 @ 5000rpm	162 @ 5500rpm
crankshaft		
no of bearings	4	4
main bearing	2½in (63.5mm) diameter	2½in (63.5mm) diameter
big end	2ins (51mm diameter)	2ins (51mm diameter)
crankcase capacity	15 pints (8.5 litres)	2 galls (9.1 litres)
cooling system	water pump, thermostat bypass, capacity 3 galls (13.6 litres)	water pump, thermostat bypass, capacity 3 galls (13.6 litres)
ignition details	Lucas, coil, 12 volts	Lucas, coil, 12 volts
ignition timing	5° btdc	5° btdc
contact breaker gap	.012in	.012in
plugs – make/gap	KLG P10 L80 10mm/ .022in	KLG F80 14mm/ n/a
carburettors	Twin SU 1¾in HV6	Twin SU 1¾in H6
fuel pump	Twin SU electric	Twin SU electric
clutch	Borg & Beck single plate type 9A6G	Borg & Beck single-plate
engine number location	Front of timing cover AND on bulkhead plate	Front of timing cover AND on bulkhead plate
Gearbox		
type	David Brown 4-speed	David Brown 4-speed
gear ratios	3.77, 5.01, 7.45 and 11.0 to 1; reverse 11.0:1	3.77 (overdrive 2.93), 5.01, 7.45 and 11.0 to 1; reverse 11.0:1
oil capacity	2¼ pints (1.3 litres)	2¼ pints (1.3 litres)

	DB2/4 Mark II	**DB Mk III**
## Chassis		
wheelbase	99in (2515mm)	99in (2515mm)
track	54in (1372mm)	54in (1372mm)
length	171½in (4356mm)	171½in (4356mm)
width	65in (1651mm)	65in (1651mm)
weight (dry)	2632lb (1194kg)	2800lb (1270kg)
turning circle	35ft (10.7m)	35ft (10.7m)
suspension	Independent at front, live axle at rear, coil springs all round	Independent at front, live axle at rear, coil springs all round
wheels and tyres	Dunlop centre-lock wires, 6.00 x 16in	Dunlop centre-lock wires, 6.00 x 16in
tyre pressures	26psi front, 27psi rear (30/31psi for high speed driving)	26psi front, 27psi rear (normal)
brakes	Girling 2LS hydraulic, drums 12in diameter	Girling hydraulic, 12in disc front (optional on first 100 cars), 12in Alfin drum rear
steering box	Marles worm and double roller	Marles worm and double roller
propeller shaft	Open, Hardy Spicer	Open, Hardy Spicer
rear axle	hypoid bevel, Salisbury	hypoid bevel, Salisbury
ratio	3.73:1	3.77:1 (4.09:1 with overdrive)
oil capacity	2½ pints (1.4 litres)	2½ pints (1.4 litres)
shock absorbers	Armstrong piston type hydraulic	Armstrong piston type hydraulic
petrol tank capacity	17 galls (77 litres), incl. 3 galls (14 litres) reserve	15½ galls (71 litres), incl. 3 galls (14 litres) reserve
chassis number location	Offside front of frame AND on bulkhead plate	Offside front of frame AND on bulkhead plate

Prices (excl. purchase tax)

	DB2/4 Mark II	DB Mk III
saloon	1955: £2050, 1957: £1925	1957-59: £2050
drophead coupé	1955: £2200	1957-59: £2300
fixed-head coupé	1955: £2050, 1957: £1925	1959: £2300

Numbers produced

	DB2/4 Mark II	DB Mk III
saloon	145	459
drophead coupé	16	85
fixed-head coupé	34	5
other	4	2
Total	199	551

Chapter Seven

The DB3 and DB3S

The DB3 and its successor the DB3S were designed from the outset as sports-racing cars, and thus only had a peripheral impact on the Aston Martin company's mainstream models. Nevertheless a certain number were sold to private buyers, and although these are largely used today only for competition, they were and are capable of being made "street legal" and used on public roads. The two models therefore merit a chapter of their own, not only for this reason but also because they had a disproportionate effect in building up the company's sporting image.

As we have seen, the seeds of the DB3 development were sown early on by David Brown, who actively encouraged company participation in racing and believed strongly in the value of competition success in promoting sales. After the initial participation of the DB1 in races during 1948 and 1949, Brown realised that the company's efforts would have to be organised around a permanent racing department under the direction of a competent full-time manager. This decision led directly to the appointment of John Wyer as racing manager in early 1950. In the short time available Wyer did what he could to make that year's cars as competitive as possible, and the DB2s duly competed at Le Mans, Spa, Silverstone and the Tourist Trophy. However, it must have been he who had a great deal to do with the arrival in November of that year of Robert Eberan von Eberhorst, to take up the position of Chief Engineer. Although von Eberhorst had a number of projects to progress, including the upgrading of the 2.6-litre

engine, Wyer would have had no doubt that the most urgent was the project known from the beginning as "DB3" – a specialised sports-racing car, designed to win races.

What Wyer, and no doubt Brown, wanted was a car which could take part in the next season's events, particularly Le Mans. However, since the design work did not get under way until January 1951, and Le Mans took place in June, there was very little time to produce the new car. For a hands-on, "can do" manager like Wyer it must have seemed at least feasible. For a perfectionist engineer like von Eberhorst it must have looked impossible from the outset; his approach was to move forward in small steps, testing each one as he went, which Wyer found frustratingly slow. Wyer, as we have already seen, prepared two new DB2s for Le Mans, but clung to the hope that at least one DB3 might be ready as well. When he realised that it was not to be so, he brought out of retirement the previous year's class-winning car and updated it – so successfully that it won its class a second time.

Delays to the DB3 prototype continued, not helped by a strike at Feltham during which the body had to be smuggled out of the works to be completed. Eventually the car (DB3/1, YMT 124) was finished in early September, which left just enough time to enter it in the Tourist Trophy at Dundrod, Northern Ireland, which was to take place on 15 September. There had not even been time to paint it when John Wyer and Lance Macklin took it for its one and only day's testing at the Motor Industry Research Association track, where a problem with oil loss from the final drive was solved by modifications to the breathing system. The car was then shipped to Belfast and hand-painted when it arrived.

Eberhorst's design parameters were four-fold. He was required to reduce the car's weight compared with the DB2, reduce its frontal area, make the frame strong enough to support open bodywork and yet provide roadholding at least as good as the DB2's. His result bore strong resemblances to the DB2, yet in many areas he had designed from scratch. Nowhere was this more true than with the chassis, which is fabricated from large-diameter round tubing, in chromium molybdenum steel, rather than the square and rectangular tubes used on the DB2. Furthermore it is in ladder form, gaining its beam strength from the tubes themselves rather than having to use a vertical girder structure. The sidemembers and centre cross-member are of 14-gauge 4in diameter material, while the front and rear crossmembers are each of 12-gauge 5in tube. There is a short rear extension made up of small-section round and rectangular tubes. The wheelbase is six inches (15cm) shorter than the DB2 at 93in (236cm).

The front suspension again bears some resemblance to the DB2 in that it uses pairs of trailing arms (contrary to the wishes of Harold Beach, who would have preferred wishbones, but von Eberhorst was insistent). However it differs in using torsion bars as the springing medium rather than coil springs. These are placed transversely within the front tubular chassis member, not unlike the anti-roll bar of the DB2. Since the torsion bars cross over each other within the chassis tube, they are not exactly in line with the rotational axis of the lower suspension arm. Each anchorage therefore takes the form of a square bronze block with radiused sides, internally splined to receive the bar, which adjusts itself through a small angular movement to line up with the axis of the bar. The lower suspension arms are mounted, as with the DB2, on needle roller bearings, while the upper arms – each in the form of a wide-spread triangular member, to resist side loads – again use the Armstrong piston-type shock-absorbers as their pivot-points. The two upper arms are connected by an anti-roll bar.

The rear suspension is totally new and is – not surprisingly in view of Eberhorst's background – reminiscent of pre-war Auto Union paractice. It uses the De Dion principle, whereby the final drive

is mounted on the chassis and is therefore part of the sprung weight, while the wheel hubs are welded to a tubular axle beam which holds the wheels parallel to each other. Axle control is via fabricated trailing arms, together with a Panhard rod for lateral location. The lower trailing arms are arranged to twist with relative movement of the De Dion tube, thus providing a degree of roll resistance. The rear brake drums are mounted inboard, connected to the final drive by short shafts, and the drive to each wheel thereafter takes the form of a splined, universally-jointed shaft. Again, von Eberhorst elected to use torsion bars as the springing medium, mounted across the chassis, but this time they lie parallel to one another, thus avoiding the need for an aligning block; to achieve this the rubber-bushed pivots of the trailing arms are closer together on the right side than on the left.

Chassis DB3/2 – the only DB3 built from new with full touring equipment. It was originally David Brown's personal car.

The De Dion rear axle of the DB3, showing the trailing arm suspension and inboard brake drums.

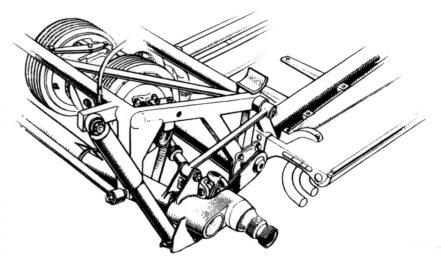

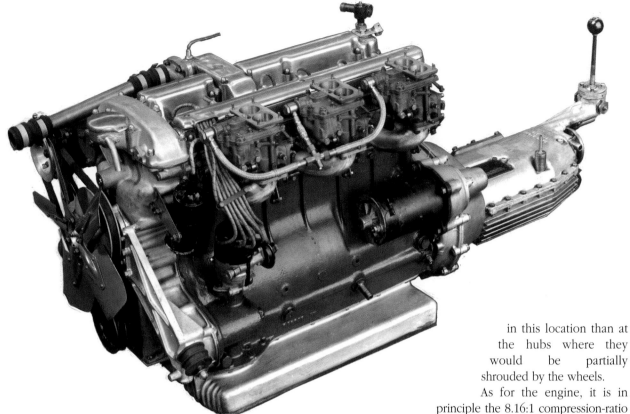

DB3 engine with triple, twin-choke downdraught Weber carburettors and five-speed gearbox.

Damping at the rear is provided by Armstrong telescopic dampers, inclined inwards at their upper mounting points.

There are other changes affecting the chassis. Steering is now by rack and pinion instead of worm and roller, and the steering column has a universal joint at the pinion end. Brakes, by Girling, use Alfin drums as standard (these later became available as an option on the DB2/4); they are of light-alloy construction with steel liners bonded in by a proprietary process. Drum dimensions are 13in (330mm) diameter by 2½in (63mm) wide at the front and 11in (280mm) by 2¼in (57mm) at the rear. The braking system is divided into two, with separate master cylinders for front and back and a simple adjustment mechanism to vary the split of braking force. Cooling of the inboard rear drums was perceived to be of critical importance, and there are scoops in the undershield which direct air to this region. Wyer was known to be concerned on this score from the outset, but he was outvoted by the experts (von Eberhorst and Pomeroy) who were convinced that it would actually be easier to cool the brake drums

in this location than at the hubs where they would be partially shrouded by the wheels.

As for the engine, it is in principle the 8.16:1 compression-ratio Vantage engine, then being offered as an option on the DB2, but there are certain modifications. The twin SU carburettors are replaced by triple dual-choke 35mm Webers, which were already known to give a substantial power increase in the DB2. Another change is the fitting of a twin exhaust system; together these two modifications raised the output of the Vantage engine from 125 to 140bhp. An oil cooler was added to the water radiator, and since the radiator was mounted much lower it was necessary to add a separate header tank. The sump was redesigned in Elektron, and this was soon to lead to problems. The engine drove through a conventional 9in (23cm) Borg & Beck clutch to a newly-designed five-speed gearbox, which was no larger or heavier than the DB2's four-speed version.

The body, by Frank Feeley, is a light structure using 18-gauge alloy panels and does not contribute to the overall strength of the car. It was designed to be lifted off the chassis quickly – in about 20 minutes – for ease of access, and comes away complete with the scuttle and wiring harness, with only the instrument drives needing disconnection. In order to give it some means of attachment, Feeley had first to design an undershield as a completely separate unit. "The underpan was a complete sub-assembly in alloy which also had to accommodate the exhaust system", Feeley recalled, "As usual the chassis designers hadn't thought about that, nor indeed how the seats were to be fixed! I wanted a clean underside to the body so I insisted the exhaust came out the side under the driver's door in a recess in the underpan". The upper body is attached to this underpan by 10 bolts, and is a minimalist structure which does little more than control the airflow round the car. It has no creature comforts such as hood, windscreen or interior trim, although these were offered as extras when the car went on sale to the public.

The car's sporting intentions are underlined by a 32-gallon (145-litre) fuel tank, mounted on the chassis rather than on the body. The stated weight, in racing trim and with nine gallons of fuel, is 18cwt (914kg), which coupled with the 140bhp output gives a bhp per tonne figure of 152 – well above the 104bhp/tonne of a Vantage-engined DB2. So it was with some degree of confidence in the design, although perhaps less in the amount of testing, that Macklin in the one and only DB3 joined the two DB2s driven by Abecassis and Shaw Taylor for the Tourist Trophy in September 1951.

Practice was encouraging, the DB3 recording fourth fastest time behind the three works Jaguar C-types. In the race Macklin seemed to be doing well for 16 laps, holding second place to Moss's Jaguar and first in class, until a bolt dropped out of the exhaust system. Once this had been fixed he rejoined the race, but on lap 27 more serious trouble arrived in the form of engine bearing failure following loss of oil. The expansion of the Elektron sump relative to the crankcase had worked the securing bolts loose and caused the cork gasket to fail.

The winter of 1951-52 was an opportunity to re-examine the DB3's design and perfect it for the coming season. This culminated in a test session with the DB3/1 prototype at the Monthléry circuit near Paris, where a De Dion tube broke. Investigation showed that it had failed in torsion, owing to the rear trailing arms not being exactly aligned with the centre-line of the chassis, which helped to explain the "twitchy" handling which the team had been experiencing. At this period there was also some experimentation with 36mm downdraught Webers, but it was soon decided to revert to the original carburettors.

The car's first public appearance in 1952 was at the BARC meeting at Goodwood in April, when motorcycle ace Geoff Duke, in his car-racing debut, came third in the prototype DB3/1. A week later Dennis Poore took DB3/2 (destined to become David Brown's personal car) to victory in a minor race at Ibsley, but a more prominent appearance was at the BRDC Silverstone meeting the following month. Wyer entered a team of four

Geoff Duke in the prototype DB3/1 at Silverstone in May 1952.

Duke at work in the prototype once again, this time in the 1952 Isle of Man Empire Trophy race where he broke the sports-car lap record.

cars, driven by Abecassis, Duke, Macklin and Parnell, using the experimental downdraught carburettors and also a different gearbox with a closer overdrive top ratio (0.885:1 instead of 0.83). Although Duke eventually retired after spinning on oil and damaging his steering, the other three, in the order Parnell-Abecassis-Macklin, came in second to fourth overall behind Moss in his C-type Jaguar. The DB3s also took the first three places in their class and won the team prize.

Next in Wyer's plans for the season was a team appearance at the Monaco Grand Prix at the beginning of June, which for that year was for sports cars. However in the meantime he entered DB3/1, with Duke driving, for the Empire Trophy on the Isle of Man. In the race Duke managed to pass Hamilton's C-type Jaguar to take the lead, and broke the sports-car lap record, before having to come into the pits with a broken ignition lead. "Ignition trouble" was the official reason for his eventual retirement, but in reality he had rejoined the race and then suffered a broken crankshaft.

Meanwhile attention was on the Monaco cars, as all three had been fitted with the new 2.9-litre engine. However, as we have already noted, this was the first engine with staggered bores, and the misalignment was initially counteracted by offsetting the small end of the connecting rod, which induced a bending load in the rod. The result was that all three cars – driven by Collins, Macklin and Parnell – retired with broken con-rods, only Collins lasting sufficient distance to be classed as a finisher (he was awarded seventh place). Parnell's exit from the race, in DB3/3, was spectacular: he spun on his own oil and caused a huge multi-car pile-up.

The DB3's less than outstanding debut season continued when the three cars moved on directly to Le Mans, joined by DB3/1 which had been fitted with an experimental hardtop body. Although Wyer played safe and flew out new 2.6-litre engines, trouble developed elsewhere. One of the open cars crashed in practice and had to be replaced by Parnell's Monaco car, hastily repaired; then in the race itself all three cars had to retire.

On two of them the final drive failed, for obscure reasons but thought to be a faulty batch of gears; this was particularly galling for the Macklin-Collins car, as it was lying fourth after twenty hours running. The third car suffered problems with its gearbox and water pump. After this experience the specification reverted to the four-speed gearbox previously developed for the lightweight DB2. In this form DB3s driven by Abecassis and Parnell came third and fourth in the Jersey Road Races, and Parnell won his class in the Boreham 100-mile race.

The next and last major event in the 1952 season was the Goodwood Nine-Hours race in August. The interval had given the team enough time to redesign the 2.9-litre engine so that the offset on the connecting-rod was at the big end, and to prepare one such car – DB3/3, to be driven by Parnell and Thompson – for the race. There had also been an upgrade to the crankshaft specification, which now called for EN25 steel instead of EN9 to give better control of the induction hardening process. This bigger engine, with the horizontal Webers, was now producing 163bhp. Two other cars with 2.6-litre engines – DB3/4 and /5, for Abecassis-Poore and Collins-Griffith – were

also entered. Although the larger-engined car retired after a disastrous fire in the pits, and the Abecassis-Poore car also retired with clutch trouble, Peter Collins and Pat Griffith went on to win the race outright, beating both the C-type Jaguars and two private Ferraris.

Only now, would it appear, did the company turn its attention towards selling the DB3 to the general public. In June the first full descriptions of the car had appeared in the motoring press, coupled with the announcement that a production run of 25 cars had been authorised. (In the event 10 were produced, and only five of these were sold new to private buyers). It was made clear that the DB3 was an addition to the range and that there was no intention that it should replace the DB2. In the run-up to the 1952 Motor Show there was a routine announcement that the DB3 would "continue unchanged" for the next season, but no price was mentioned. From other sources a tax-inclusive price of £3700 was quoted, which compared with £2724 and £2879 for the DB2 saloon and drophead coupé respectively.

Although no formal road test of the DB3 was carried out while it was new, in October 1952

George Abecassis in DB3/4 at Boreham in August 1952.

works driver George Abecassis gave readers of the upmarket British magazine *The Field* his impressions of driving the car, both on the road and on the Monthléry circuit. It is unclear whether the performance figures he quoted were his own or whether, more likely, he was using factory data. For the record, he talked of rest to 100mph in 22 seconds, a maximum speed of 130mph, and a maximum in third gear (with a five-speed gearbox) of 87mph at 5500rpm. More impressive, even in those far-off days of unlimited speeds outside towns, were his reported achievements between his central-Paris hotel and the circuit: "… as I engaged fifth at 110mph I thought I could hear my passenger gasp … on up to 125, when a cyclist far ahead caused a check down to 90; but a swift change to fourth soon brought back the speed".

Abecassis made clear to his readers that this was no luxury car. "It is made for one purpose and one purpose only, to win sports car events over any period up to twenty-four hours. The few cars that have been constructed to this date, although all identical, are in fact prototypes and largely experimental … there are just two bucket seats, that for the passenger being particularly Spartan … no carpet graces the floor … a single aero screen deflects the air over the driver's head, but any passenger must rely purely on goggles or visor." Nevertheless "all thoroughbred cars invariably give the driver, even on first acquaintance, an immediate sense of confidence", and once on the circuit. "that original sense of confidence was maintained and, if anything, increased, and I attributed this to the fact that the car has got about the right amount of understeer. With a full tank (32 gallons) and complete with driver, the weight distribution is almost exactly 50-50. This is combined with a rear axle geometry which gives some degree of roll-understeer, and the Porsche-type front suspension increases the slip angle on roll. With all these desirable features, the handling characteristics approach the ideal".

There is hardly a breath of criticism, which is understandable from someone who was on the company's payroll (and married to the boss's daughter!). The brakes, he confesses, need a heavy pedal pressure, but this is only to compensate for wear and drum expansion in long-distance races. "For road use this might easily be obviated, but only a servo, or, better still, the disc brake could restore the situation for the track." Do we detect here just a trace of envy of the C-type Jaguar's disc brakes, and a subtle plea for them on the DB3?

During the 1952-53 winter some development of the DB3 continued, including testing at the Monza track in Italy where it set a new sports-car lap record (previously held by a Mercedes 300SL). Nevertheless Wyer was disappointed to find that the DB3's dry weight with the 2.9-litre engine was now in excess of 2000lb (907kg), which was only 110lb (45kg) less than the lightweight DB2 of the previous year. Accordingly he was receptive when Willie Watson proposed another redesign to reduce weight, and the result was the DB3S. The wheelbase is reduced by a further six inches (15cm) to 87in (221cm), and the chassis tubes reduced in thickness, the sidemembers from 14- to 16-gauge and the crossmembers from 12- to 14-gauge. As a result the weight comes down to 1850lb (839kg), a reduction compared with the DB3 of 167lb (76kg).

Other changes include the deletion of the

The DB3S chassis, with its highly aerodynamic bodywork shown in outline. The wheelbase was shortened by six inches compared with the DB3.

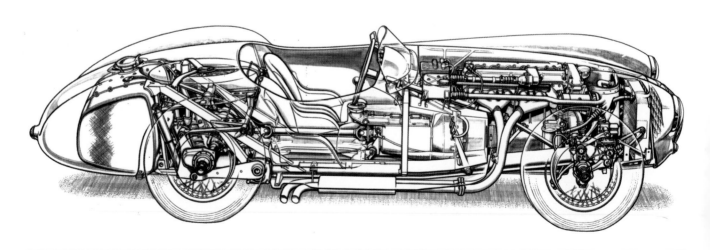

Panhard rod in favour of a quite different device to locate the De Dion axle – a Tufnol block sliding in guide plates bolted to the final drive casing. The final drive itself changes from hypoid to a spiral bevel in an attempt to eliminate the overheating problem with this component. The new unit also allows more rapid changes of ratio; its only drawback is a small increase in the height of the propeller shaft. There are improvements to the 2.9-litre engine as well, including camshafts with a five-degree longer dwell and inlet valves increased in diameter from 1.515 to 1.595in (38.5 to 40.5mm), which together raise power output by 22bhp to 182bhp. Brake drums are uprated to 13in (33cm) diameter by 2½in (64mm) wide at the front, 12in (30.5cm) by 2½in (64mm) at the rear, and the previous balance adjustment between the front and rear master cylinders is replaced by Girling automatic adjusters. The steering column now has a second universal joint.

To this chassis has been applied an elegant new body, again designed by Frank Feeley. A feature is the cutaway behind each wheel, and Feeley later recounted how this had come about. "One of the things I was always concerned about was getting rid of hot under-bonnet air that had come through the radiator. We certainly had this problem with the DB3 and had to cut vents to let it out. But it was never really fully satisfactory and when the DB3S followed I was determined to get over this problem. We had scale models made and tested them in the Vickers wind tunnel at Weybridge where they had some decent aerodynamicists. Without a doubt the wind tunnel work was useful to us and it proved that my idea for cutting away the wings behind the wheels did allow the extrac-

tion of hot air. It was certainly effective and was not simply a styling feature and it was adopted by other people later." The 18-gauge body panels are clinched to a supporting framework made from ⅜in and ½in (10mm and 12mm) diameter steel tubing, which has angle or Z-section strips welded to it where necessary to support the panels.

The development timetable for the DB3S meant that Wyer had to start the 1953 season using the previous year's DB3 cars. The opening event was the twelve-hour race at Sebring in Florida, a key venue for American sports-car buffs and an important one for the team as it was the first round of the World Sports Car Championship. The company entered two cars, for Collins-Duke (DB3/4) and

DB3/5. This is the Abecassis/Parnell car which finished second in the 1953 Sebring 12-Hours.

Minimal weather equipment could be supplied on the DB3S if necessary. Note the deep scoops behind the front wheel to extract hot under-bonnet air.

OUTRIGHT WIN FOR ASTON MARTIN

*Aston Martin DB.3s model
driven by R. Parnell.*

EMPIRE TROPHY
I.O.M.

New average and lap speed records were
established by R. Parnell in an Aston Martin
DB.3s, the outright winner.

Subject to official confirmation.

★
★
★

*For the private owner: the race-bred luxury
DB.2, sister-car to the competition DB.3s.*

ASTON MARTIN LTD · FELTHAM · MIDDLESEX
London Showrooms : 103 New Bond Street · London · W.1

A DAVID BROWN COMPANY

*The company were
advertising Parnell's
success within days
of the race.*

*Opposite: British
Empire Trophy, Isle of
Man, June 1953,
with Reg Parnell in
DB3S/1 on his way
to winning. Behind
him is Stirling Moss
in a C-Type Jaguar.*

drove on the ignition switch. The well-known
photographer Louis Klementaski had ridden with
Parnell and later described him as "pressing
pedals, changing gear with one hand, manipu-
lating the ignition switch with the other to prevent
the engine bursting, and steering with either when
he could devote his attention to that". Collins and
Abecassis both experienced broken steering-rack
mountings. Abecassis retired and Collins could
only finish sixteenth. The first four places were
filled by two Ferraris, an Alfa Romeo and a Lancia,
the Jaguar team of three C-types all having retired
before half-distance. Two weeks later it was the
BRDC Silverstone meeting, where Parnell's DB3/3
now had the 182bhp engine. He finished third
behind the two 4.1-litre Ferraris of Hawthorn and
Cole, with Collins fourth in DB3/4 in front of two
C-type Jaguars. Duke (DB3/2) suffered a clutch
problem and retired.

The DB3S was so nearly ready that Wyer decided
to enter a team of three cars for Le Mans, yet
despite a test session at Monza immediately after
the Mille Miglia the cars were prepared in a hurry.
Although the new model had a gratifying maiden
win at Charterhall in May, it had not been fully
tested when the team arrived at the circuit in June.
The three cars were DB3S/2 for Parnell-Collins,
DBS3/3 for Abecassis-Salvadori and DBS3/4 for
Poore-Thompson, all with the new, lighter gearbox
with needle-roller bearings. All three retired from
the race – Parnell on lap 16 after a crash (his fault,
he admitted), the Abecassis-Salvadori car on lap 73
with a clutch problem, and the Poore-Thompson
car on lap 182 with an engine blow-up. Although
the team could hardly have expected miracles with
a new car, these results were disappointing, but
thereafter things improved, and as things turned
out the DB3S won every remaining race for which
it was entered in 1953.

First came a lone entry for Parnell in the prototype, DB3S/1, in the British Empire Trophy in the
Isle of Man. He duly won, making atonement for
his mistake at Le Mans, and beating a Frazer Nash,
a Ferrari and three Jaguars. Then came the July
Silverstone meeting, where the team came in first,
second and third overall. Parnell won after a duel
with Rolt in a C-type Jaguar which ended when
Rolt pitted with a cracked piston. Next was the
Goodwood Nine-Hours race, where the Parnell-
Thompson car won with Collins and Griffith
second, the Salvadori-Poore car having retired with
a con-rod failure. The DB3Ss had beaten off a
strong challenge from no less than four C-type

Abecassis-Parnell (DB3/5), both with the larger
2.9-litre engine although still at the 160bhp state of
tune. The two crews suffered from the number of
relatively inexperienced drivers on the course, and
both were involved in collisions. The Collins-Duke
car had to retire, but Abecassis and Parnell
managed to continue (with only one headlamp),
finishing second overall to a 5.4-litre Cunningham
and first in their class. However, it was yet another
case of bad luck for the team and could so easily
have ended with an overall win.

Next was the Mille Miglia, and a four-car entry
once again included a DB2 driven by Wisdom. A
fifth place for Parnell was a satisfactory result,
especially as his car had suffered from a broken
Panhard rod. It also transpired that Parnell had
driven the final part of the course with no accelerator control; instead he tied the throttle open and

DB3S/4, the winning Collins/ Griffith car, at the Ulster Tourist Trophy in September 1953.

Plenty of atmosphere in this shot of the works team cars at Sebring in March 1954. Left to right: Parnell/Salvadori, Collins/Griffith, Shelby/Wallace.

Jaguars, all of which apparently succumbed to oil-surge problems. Finally came the Tourist Trophy at Dundrod, where the Goodwood positions were reversed, Collins and Griffith winning and Parnell and Thompson coming second. Salvadori and Poore again retired, Poore having crashed the car after he found one of his rear wheels overtaking him. The three works Jaguars had looked likely winners but all had retired with gearbox failure.

In the Tourist Trophy, Parnell, driving DB3S/2, had used an experimental set-up with the rear brakes moved outboard, and this had been successful. Wyer, it will be recalled, had always had his doubts about the inboard brakes, and his opinion had been savagely vindicated by the various troubles in this area. Not only could many

of the final-drive failures be ascribed to over-heating – almost certainly from the adjacent brake drums – but so could the fire in the pits during the 1952 Goodwood Nine-Hour race. From this point on the outboard position was standardised.

At that year's London Show there was a DB3S on the Aston Martin stand, but there was no price tag and it was made clear that the car was not yet for sale to the public. In theory the racing department should have been flat out during the winter developing the car further, to capitalise on its successful first season, but the reality was different. Since

1952 there had been a project in place to develop a new Lagonda with a V12 engine. With its 4½-litre engine this was the car Brown had always felt he needed to compete not only with Jaguar but especially with Ferrari, whose own V12 engines had now reached 4.5 litres. Willie Watson had been brought back as design engineer for the project, and by the winter of 1953-54 his efforts were coming to fruition. As a result Wyer's department – which was responsible for all production development as well as racing – was stretched beyond its capacity, and development of the DB3S suffered.

The Collins/ Griffith car, DB3S/4, in the 1954 Mille Miglia, where it failed to finish.

Moreover the planned racing programme for 1954 was even more ambitious than the previous year's, putting yet more pressure on the department. Thus the specification of the DB3S changed very little, other than the outboard rear brakes and the substitution of a three-plate clutch for the previous single-plate version, which was clearly not up to the torque now being put through it.

The racing programme began as early as January that year, with three entries in the Buenos Aires 1000-kilometre race, and finished in October at the Aintree circuit near Liverpool. In between there were the by now usual events – Sebring, Mille Miglia, Silverstone (twice), Le Mans and the Tourist Trophy. Things started badly, with one of the Buenos Aires cars crashing and killing its driver (Forrest Greene), another retiring (Parnell) and the third (Collins/Griffith) finishing third overall. The team stayed abroad for the next race, Sebring, which meant that they were short of spares and workshop facilities. Inevitably the cars suffered and all three retired. The cars arrived back at Feltham on 15 April, giving little time to prepare even the

best two before their departure for the Mille Miglia on the 24th. In that race both cars crashed and retired. At Le Mans, where the prototype V12 Lagonda was also entered, two of the four team cars crashed and two retired with mechanical problems. The second Silverstone meeting did at least see the three cars in the first three places.

In spite of the pressures on the development personnel, a number of significant improvements were introduced during the season. Raising the compression ratio to 9.4:1 on the Buenos Aires cars had produced another 14bhp, bringing the power output to 194bhp. Then at Silverstone in May the cars ran with a new design of aluminium head which accommodated both twin 10mm spark plugs and larger valves – 1.75in (44mm) inlet, 1.55in (39mm) exhaust. Coupled with an increase in maximum revolutions from 5500 to 6000rpm, this lifted the output to 225bhp. The same event saw the first appearance of fixed-head coupé bodies on two new chassis, DB3S/6 and /7. Wind-tunnel tests had suggested that these would produce a higher maximum speed, but the predictions were not

The V-12 Lagonda which took part in the 1954 Le Mans 24-Hours. The concentration of development time on this project hampered work on improving the DB3S.

borne out in practice, and the cars' handling was also adjudged slightly worse. When both bodies were written off in crashes at Le Mans there was no move to replace them. The same Silverstone meeting also saw the first use of disc brakes, of Lockheed manufacture, which were fitted at the front of the prototype car DB3S/1. (Interestingly, the drivers still preferred to retain the drum brakes for some races.) Finally, this same car at Le Mans ran with an experimental supercharger and a single 52mm Weber carburettor, producing 240bhp.

The London Earls Court Motor Show in October 1954 at last saw the DB3S officially on sale to the public at an eye-watering £2600 basic or £3684 including tax. The specification offered was an 8.5:1 compression ratio, iron-head engine with triple twin-choke Solex carburettors, producing 180bhp at 5500rpm. The latest needle-roller

Start of the 1954 Le Mans race. Number 8 (second from left) is the Parnell/ Salvadori car, which retired.

DB3S/6 at Silverstone, May 1954, the first appearance of the fixed-head coupé body designed for Le Mans that year. British racegoing attire of the period is also well illustrated.

The fixed-head coupé DB3S/6 again, this time in action at Le Mans; drivers were Collins and Bira. Both this car and its twin crashed, destroying the bodies (to most people's satisfaction).

bearing four-speed gearbox was included but not disc brakes, only Alfin drums. The company publicity talked rather optimistically of "a maximum speed approaching 150mph".

The 1955 racing season, in contrast to the previous year, was reasonably successful. It started with Parnell coming third with DB3S/5 (using an experimental 2½-litre engine) in the Empire Trophy at Oulton Park, then saw Collins blow up his

engine in the same car in the Mille Miglia. However the one-hour race at Silverstone was quite a triumph: two brand-new cars, DB3S/6 and /7, were entered for Parnell and Salvadori and finished first and second respectively, convincingly beating the D-Type Jaguars in the process. The cars had been improved in several ways over the winter, with a ZF limited slip differential and uprated final drive (using the specification developed for the V12

Lagonda project), disc brakes all round and a 12-plug engine. Their superiority over the 1954 cars entered for Collins and Walker was clear, those cars finishing seventh and eighth respectively.

The following day Paul Frère in DB3S/8 (another new car, but running without the benefit of the 12-plug head) won at Spa, beating two Ferrari 500 Monzas and a C-Type Jaguar. At Le Mans Collins and Frère came second and won their class,

although the Salvadori and Brooks cars both had to retire. At the Aintree British GP meeting four cars (including /5, now brought up to the latest specification) filled the first four places, with Hawthorn's D-Type Jaguar coming behind in fifth. The Goodwood Nine-Hours Race saw a win for the third year in succession. Walker and Poore in DB3S/7 beat off three 750 Monza Ferraris and a D-type Jaguar to finish first, with Collins and Brooks

This is DB3S/119, one of the rare fixed-head coupés on the DB3S chassis.

in DB3S/6 in third place. The International Trophy at Oulton Park followed on, and again saw the cars finish first (Parnell) and third (Collins), while the season's final event, the Tourist Trophy, gained a fourth place for the team (Walker/Poore) behind three Mercedes 300SLRs. In this race Collins (who after a delayed start was running third at one point before retiring) was using an experimental 2992 cc engine with ultra-thin wall liners to give an 84mm bore instead of 83.

The D-Type Jaguar with its larger engine was a close competitor on the track. The DB3Ss could often beat them, but not at Le Mans

At the 1955 London Show the DB3S was again on offer to the public, unchanged in price at £2600 basic but with a major improvement to the specification in that the power output had gone up considerably. Compared with the previous year's 180bhp at 5500rpm it was now variously given as 207bhp and 210bhp at 6000rpm, ascribed to a modified cylinder head. Although this would still have been the cast-iron head rather than the aluminium version fitted to the works cars, there had apparently been a slight increase in compression ratio from 8.5:1 to 8.68:1. Part of the improvement in power will also have come from the increase in permitted revolutions.

In February 1956 there at last came a road test of the DB3S. This was in *Autosport* and was conducted by their swashbuckling staffer John Bolster. His quoted output figure was also 210bhp at 6000rpm, although he only used the maximum revolutions to obtain his top speed (140.6mph) and otherwise restrained himself to 5500rpm in the intermediate gears. Even so, acceleration times of 6.6sec from rest to 60mph and 14.4sec to 100mph were remarkable – the best set of figures ever recorded by the magazine at that time. His car, like

A wet (and sad) 1955 Le Mans. The Collins/Frère car, DB3S/6 - now with open bodywork - finished second overall and first in its class.

Aintree, July 1955 – the British Grand Prix meeting. At the start of the sports-car race Salvadori (3) leads Collins (1), and they finished in that order.

1955 Goodwood 9-hours: the Collins/ Brooks car which finished third.

all non-works cars, had drum brakes rather than discs, but at least they were now mounted outboard. In spite of their relocation, however, it is clear that there were still concerns about the final drive overheating, since the car sported an ugly piece of air-trunking leading from the scuttle ventilator across the centre of the cabin to the area of the rear axle.

Bolster was impressed both by the car's docility in traffic and by its handling and cornering power when he took it on to a race circuit: "It is impossible to refrain from using superlatives when dealing with this side of the car's character". Like

Abecassis with the DB3, he was initially uncomfortable with the high pedal pressures needed for the brakes, but found that at higher speeds they were very powerful. In summary, "one only has to drive a thoroughbred such as this to realise that, where a low selling price is not the main objective, a more advanced chassis design can give a standard of roadholding and controllability which is beyond comparison".

In May 1956 the company announced, somewhat surprisingly, that a new body style was available, a fixed-head coupé with a fastback tail treatment. The

Start of the 1955 Goodwood 9-hours race. De Portago's Ferrari is first away, but the Walker/Poore DB3S (3) was the eventual winner.

design was said to have been "initially laid down" by David Brown himself, which probably served to underline that Frank Feeley had retired from the company. It had a detachable panel in the roof, which fitted exactly in the luggage space behind the rear seats. The DB3S was now coming to the end of its life, and these bodies could have been an attempt to sell off the remaining chassis before a formal announcement was made. At the same time the company lent one of the coupés to Laurence Pomeroy of *The Motor* for evaluation; this was DB3S/120, registered 58 JHX, and was David Brown's personal car.

Pomeroy spent his allotted space musing over the extent to which racing had contributed to the car's characteristics, and understandably came to the conclusion that it had done so greatly. Along the way he commented on how small the car felt, and how it would cruise easily at 80mph, "with a quick leap to three figures whenever a clear stretch came in sight". He was also impressed with the car's smoothness and quietness, compared with the Mercedes-Benz 300SLR which he had just been driving, and of course with its roadholding. "One

has a sense of absolute accuracy when cornering and there is appreciable understeer in these conditions despite the almost extreme sensitivity to movement of the steering wheel." On the other hand he noticed a tendency to wander at around 120mph, which – presciently, for this was a relatively unexplored phenomenon at the time – he laid at the door of the car's aerodynamics.

The 1956 season was again moderately successful for the DB3S, but increasingly the development effort was being concentrated on its successor, the DBR1, a model which would never be offered to the public. Nevertheless certain improvements were introduced, notably a move to dry-sump lubrication as a means of lowering the car's profile, accompanied by redesigned bodywork with a lower nose. Sebring brought a fourth place and first in class, at a speed faster than the previous year's overall winner. The cars gained first and second at the May Silverstone meeting, and Moss (now leading the team) came second at the Rouen Grand Prix. At Le Mans, which was also the first race for the new DBR1, the Moss/Collins DB3S/9 came second to the Ecurie Ecosse Jaguar and first in its class.

By late 1955 the Mercedes 300SLR, here seen with air brake raised, was presenting a formidable threat to the Aston Martins.

The Silverstone Daily Express meeting in 1956. Moss finished second in DB3S/8, behind Salvadori in DB3S/5

Sure enough, the official announcement that the DB3S was going out of production came at the beginning of October 1956. A total of 31 cars had been produced, of which 12 were works cars and the remaining 19 had been sold to private owners.

Both the DB3 and the DB3S had shown great promise at times, but lack of time and resources had caused the company to lose the initiative and fail to turn promise into achievement. It would take these cars' successors, the DBR series, to do that.

Le Mans 1956. The Moss/Collins DB3S/9 (number 8) finished second overall and first in class.

These photos show the former team car DB3S/9. In 1956 Stirling Moss was leading the team, and he and Peter Collins finished second at Le Mans that year.

Collins also led the Rouen GP that same year in this car until he was forced to retire. In 1957 the car went to Australia where it notched up further competition successes

THE DB3 AND DB3S

149

Summary Statistics

	DB3	**DB3S**
Engine		
configuration	6 cylinders in line, overhead valves, twin overhead camshafts	6 cylinders in line, overhead valves, twin overhead camshafts
capacity	2580cc	2922cc
bore	83mm	78mm
stroke	90mm	90mm
RAC rating	22.6hp	25.6hp
compression ratio	8.16:1	8.68:1
firing order	153624	153624
valve timing	n/a	io 2° btdc, eo 7° atdc
tappet clearances (cold)	inlet .010in, exhaust .015in	inlet .010in, exhaust .015in
brake horsepower	140 @ 5500rpm	210 @ 6000rpm
crankshaft		
no of bearings	4	4
main bearing	2½in (63.5mm) diameter	2½in (63.5mm) diameter
big end	2ins (51mm diameter)	2ins (51mm diameter)
crankcase capacity	3 galls (13.6 litres)	3 galls (13.6 litres)
cooling system	water pump, thermostat bypass, capacity 3 galls (13.6 litres)	water pump, thermostat bypass, capacity 3 galls (13.6 litres)
ignition details	Lucas, coil, 12 volts	Lucas, coil, 12 volts
ignition timing	n/a	10° btdc
contact breaker gap	.012in	.012in
plugs - make/gap	KLG P10 L80 10mm	KLG 10mm: P10 L80 (touring), T240/3 (racing)/ .015in
carburettors	Triple 36DCF5 dual-choke Weber downdraught	Triple 40DCO 3 dual-choke Weber
fuel pump	Twin SU electric	
clutch	Borg & Beck single plate, 9in hydraulic	9in single plate
engine number location	Front of timing cover AND on bulkhead plate	Front of timing cover AND on bulkhead plate
Gearbox		
type	Early: David Brown S527 5-speed; Later: S430 4-speed	David Brown S430/12 4-speed
gear ratios	Early: 3.415, 4.11, 5.24, 7.768 and 11.919 to 1; reverse 8.63:1. Later: 3.73, 4.69, 6.97 and 10.88 to 1; reverse 10.88:1	3.73, 4.69, 6.97 and 10.88 to 1; reverse 10.88:1
Chassis		
wheelbase	93in (2362mm)	87in (2210mm)
track	51in (1295mm)	49in (1245mm)
length	158½ins (4026mm)	154ins (3912mm) [fixed-head coupé 156½ins (3975mm)]
width	61½in (1562mm)	59in (1500mm)
weight (dry)	1893lb (858kg)	1940lb (880kg)
turning circle	32ft (9.75mm)	30ft (9.14m)
suspension	independent at front, de Dion at rear, torsion bars all round	independent at front, de Dion at rear, torsion bars all round
wheels and tyres	Dunlop centre-lock wires, 6.00 x 16in	Dunlop centre-lock wires, 6.00 x 16in
tyre pressures	28psi all round	
brakes	Girling 2LS hydraulic, Alfin drums, 13in dia front, 11in dia (inboard) rear	Girling 2LS hydraulic, Alfin drums, 13in dia front, 12in dia rear
steering box	Rack and pinion	Rack and pinion
rear axle	Hypoid bevel, de Dion axle	Spiral bevel, de Dion axle
ratio	Early 4.11:1, later 3.73:1	3.73:1
shock absorbers	Armstrong - front IS10 piston type, rear AT7 telescopic	
petrol tank capacity	32 galls (146 litres)	35 galls (159 litres), incl. 5 galls (23 litres) reserve [fixed-head coupé: 28¼ galls(129 litres)]
chassis number location	Bulkhead plate AND rear jacking-point	
Prices (excl. purchase tax)		
fixed-head coupé	1954: £3200	
open sports	1952: £2465	1954: £2600
Numbers Produced		
fixed-head coupé		3
open sports	10	28
Total	10	31

Chapter Eight

On the road then

Looking back over a span of 50 years, it is hard for us to imagine just how sensational a DB2 Aston Martin must have seemed to the ordinary British motorist of those days. Its performance figures can be matched or exceeded today by many versions of the Ford Focus or Peugeot 206, so to drive one now, although an interesting experience, is not truly a mind-blowing one. What we tend to forget is the relentless pace of development which has taken place in the intervening time, and how what is normal today was near to unimaginable for most car owners then.

When the DB2 was launched in 1950, a typical motorist – if he could afford a new car at all – might well have aspired to, say, a Morris Minor. This attractive little car, renowned at the time for its handling, had a 918cc sidevalve engine which gave it a maximum speed of 62mph; the time it took to accelerate from rest to 60mph was too long to be recorded. Even at the end of the DB2's life – 1959, when the DB Mark III was just going out of production – the average car was still a pretty slow beast. It was in the spring of that year that the Triumph Herald was launched; its 948cc pushrod ohv engine propelled it from rest to 60mph in 30 seconds, and it achieved a top speed of 70 miles per hour. Later that year came the "New Anglia" from Ford, with its unusual reverse-slope rear window; here was a

Ford's "New Anglia" was contemporary with the DB Mark III, but 0-60mph took 29 seconds.

Morris Oxford: 78mph maximum against 138mph for a DB3S.

little more performance, with a 0-60mph time of 29 seconds and a maximum of 77mph.

Even moving up a size did not make a dramatic difference: the latest ("Farina") versions of the Austin A55 Cambridge and Morris Oxford could only achieve 78mph. When drivers of these cars saw an Aston Martin in their mirrors they moved over quickly, if only to enjoy, briefly, the sight of a car which had three times their acceleration and a top speed half as fast again. In theory these speed differentials exist on a higher plane today: our Ford Focus might take 30 seconds to reach 100mph, while the Aston Martin Vanquish needs only 10. The difference, of course, is that such speeds today are illegal in most countries, and therefore the comparison breaks down. On the British roads of 50 years ago to have this crushing acceleration available for passing slower cars was to move into another world.

Now and again we are allowed a quick glimpse of the road conditions which prevailed in those days. As late as 1956, when Maurice Smith, editor of *The Autocar*, and a passenger leave Feltham in a DB3S and head for Silverstone, "we bowl along in the slow traffic stream towards London Airport at 25mph in third gear". So if this is bowling along, we ask ourselves, how slow would a crawl be?

Earlier, at the start of the 1950s, things would have been even more tedious. Petrol rationing only finished in that year, Britain was still in an austerity mood, and with a serious shortage of new cars for the home market most vehicles on the road were survivors from the 1930s. This was a period, therefore, when getting the old bus up to 50 miles per hour was regarded as making rapid progress.

At least in urban and suburban areas, the traffic speeds which the average motorist accepted in 1950 would not only be painfully slow today, but were already so to the owner of a DB2. His frustration at the Ford 8s and Austin Rubys in front of him would not have been greeted with sympathy. Indeed the very idea of buying a supercar in the early postwar period was offensive to some people, since they resented those who had managed to hold on to or even increase their wealth during the war. Not that there were too many British buyers queuing up for a DB2 in 1950; this, as well as government pressure to protect the balance of payments, explains the very high proportion which were exported.

Once our two *Autocar* journalists and their DB3S were out of town, things were different, even as late as 1956. "As we left Aylesbury on the Bicester road I murmured a short prayer for a clear part on the long straight a few miles ahead … My luck was out to start with, but after the little humped bridge there were only a few fast-moving vehicles which the Aston mopped up at about 90mph. At last, ahead and clear, lay the best and widest stretch. Here was the hoped-for opportunity and it was right foot hard down … Even in these blasé days, 138mph (as recorded by my passenger) is no mean speed on an English road." Legal considerations apart, there are very few A-roads today where the traffic would allow such a speed to be attained.

Smith was probably lucky to find such an open stretch of road. Only three years later we find Salvadori, testing the DB Mark III, complaining that such conditions no longer existed. "When it came to attempting high-speed runs I was hampered by the all too familiar excessive amount of traffic, often behaving in an erratic fashion, and the apparent impossibility of finding a really long stretch of road with no unforeseen hazards." In fact the car's top speed was fast becoming academic in Britain – it was its acceleration which made the difference. An earlier (1954) road test had summed up the situation well: "The out-of-date road system of this country is the limiting factor for a car of this

potency and, because of these restrictions, the acceleration capabilities of the Aston Martin are so valuable. The average time for a familiar journey can be cut by a large margin, mainly by virtue of the ease and safety with which slow moving vehicles can be overtaken. On a number of occasions during the test three-figure speeds were seen on the exceptionally accurate speedometer and these were very quickly reached through the wonderful surge of power available in the lower ratios, and without annoyance to other road users".

Those lucky few Britons who could afford a DB2, and who were able to get hold of one, were of course totally enthusiastic about the car. Rob Walker, for example, best known as a Formula One entrant but a highly skilled driver as well, persuaded the company in 1951 to sell him one of the 1950 works cars, VMF 65. This had the twin benefits of a Vantage high-compression engine and suspension which had been very carefully set up. Writing a few months after he had acquired the car, Rob wrote that it was "the most marvellous car of its type in the world, and to me it is the perfect dream car … I think the thing that delights me most about the DB2 is the way that you can amble

Aston Martin works driver Brian Shaw-Taylor rated the Lancia Aprilia his favourite car until he drove the DB2.

comfortably through traffic at 20mph in top gear and then accelerate away, but if you get a short open stretch all you need do is go down into second and she will climb straight up to 75mph and from there in third she will go up to about 96 or 100mph. Another amazement is that you never hear the engine at all; it is completely smooth and the only thing that can be heard is a somewhat noisy exhaust. When I bought the Aston Martin I was quite prepared to scoff at it, having had excellent and very fast French cars, but as can be seen I have changed my tune, and have no hesitation in saying that it is the finest car to drive that I have ever owned".

Brian Shaw-Taylor was another expert driver who had a high opinion of the DB2. In this case he was not an owner, but he spoke with the authority of one who had been a works driver in the 1951 team, co-driving both at Le Mans and in the Tourist Trophy. At the time his daily car was a Lancia Aprilia, which he very much admired. "There is

only one car which I would swap the Aprilia for and that is a DB2 Aston Martin, and even that is limited by having no room for a proper rear seat. The roadholding of the DB2 is, in my opinion, unbeatable. A great deal of talk goes on these days about over- and under-steer. The DB2 does neither. The front and rear (at racing speed) break away equally, so that the whole car shifts bodily across the road according to the speed at which a bend is taken. The steering wheel can be turned to a fixed amount and then left alone. Perfect!"

One thing that the experts – competition drivers and road-testers – agreed on was this matter of balance in the DB2's roadholding. When Shaw-Taylor refers to the front and rear "breaking away equally" he is echoing the comments of *The Motor*: "The car as a whole will slide its tail outwards in a gentle and easily manageable manner when pushed by excessive power beyond the limits of adhesion on either wet or dry roads". John Bolster, testing the car for *Autosport*, used the racing parl-

Private owners used their DB2s in sports car races; this is Goodwood in 1952, with two Healey Silverstones and a distressing number of Jaguars ahead of the Aston Martin.

ance of the time when he referred to the "four wheel drift technique". This was a phenomenon which is difficult to reproduce these days, other than at racing speeds on a closed circuit. The reason is that both road surfaces and, particularly, tyres have improved dramatically in the intervening time; in 1951 there was no such thing as a radial tyre, and crossplies lost adhesion much earlier.

American testers were just as conscious of the DB2's ability to be "drifted" at high speed – and so were American buyers, since in the model's early days many of them bought the car with the intention of using it in competition. Phil Hill, testing the car for *Road & Track*, was precise in his analysis. "There will be slight oversteer with the tyres soft … corrected tyre pressure finds the driver able to break the rear end loose at high speed, but the steering is so acute that a slight correction stops the skid immediately." The DB2 had a strong following in North America and elsewhere amongst racers who felt that, despite its lack of

litres compared with some competitors, it stood a good chance on the track. It has to be said, however, that the car never quite produced the results that it was capable of doing. At Sebring, in particular, there were some defeats which should have been victories, and this was especially disappointing at the most important meeting in the company's biggest market.

Perhaps if the company had given more attention to Sebring and less to, say, domestic UK races, then the its reputation, and sales, in America might have stood even higher. This applies not just to the early DB2 but also to its sporting successors, the DB3 and DB3S. The likelihood of these latter two models being purchased as everyday cars was infinitesimal, so it was even more important that the company scored some competition successes with them, particularly in North America, where there were by far the greatest number of potential buyers wanting to go racing every weekend. Yet, as we have seen, the crucial moment when the

Grand Prix driver Innes Ireland preferred the DB2/4 Aston to the Jaguar XK120, particularly its handling and brakes.

DB3S in particular was approaching greatness and needed constant development input was the very time when the company's resources were concentrated on the V12 Lagonda project.

As the years progressed the DB2 subtly evolved in character. Whereas to begin with it was virtually a sports-racer which could also be used on the road, it gradually became an iconic, aspirational object which only a few could afford and which said all that was necessary about both the owner – both his (usually his, not her) sporting character and his wealth. The racing driver and motoring journalist Innes Ireland once encapsulated his feelings about the model, and in doing so placed it precisely in the social pecking order of the time. "I would have been about twenty-six when I first drove an Aston Martin; I'd left the army, been back to Rolls-Royce for nine months – I'd already served a five-year apprenticeship with this revered company – and had started a business in partnership with a fellow apprentice. Naturally we specialised in the repair and overhaul of Rolls-Royce and Bentley cars, other exciting marques providing the spice of life. ... The Aston Martin was the property of a Harley Street specialist. It was fairly new, a DB2/4 Mk II convertible, Ferrari red in colour with a light tan hood and matching leather interior. Our garage was near the village of Elstead in Surrey, and for the convenience of customers, most of them London based, we collected and delivered their cars. My partner and I would toss a coin for the privilege of driving the Aston – I always won for we used a coin from my pocket. It was the one with two heads!

"Although I had driven an XK120 Jaguar once, I think the Aston was quicker. If it wasn't it certainly felt like it, for it handled a good deal better and at least had decent brakes. The red paintwork was always spotlessly clean and how grand I felt easing it through London's traffic heading for the open road to Guildford. Heads turned in admiration as I passed, for the glamorous beauty of an Aston Martin convertible was not a common sight; I played the part of 'owner' to the hilt, revelling in the envious stares! But it was on the open road I enjoyed the real excitement of the car, the surge of power from its three-litre engine in overtaking, maximum revs in every gear, the quick changes from one to the next, the sureness of the brakes and the well balanced feel I sensed in the corners. I always felt I was doing the owner a favour on these runs, cleaning out the car's system of the cobwebs and soot gathered from the lethargy of its normal town living."

New Riley Pathfinder at £1411 – preferable to a two-year old DB2/4 at £1895?

The Rover 75 was a high-status car, but not as high as an Aston Martin

Jaguar 2.4 – still only for junior directors, not for the top brass.

The R Type Bentley was on a par with the Aston Martin for price and status, but had a much more more conservative image

Getting into the business of servicing DB2s would have been a shrewd choice, as these cars needed constant attention to give of their best. Quite apart from the kingpins needing greasing every 1000miles – in other words, whenever you had been on a round trip from London to Scotland – not only were there 14 more points requiring greasing every 2500 miles, but at the same service you had to have a complete change of engine oil. And then there was another list of duties to perform at 5000 and 10,000 miles, not to mention the various "adjustments" which had to be carried out when necessary (such as the brakes). No wonder that a two year old DB2/4, which *The Autocar* tested in its "Used Cars on the Road" series in early 1957, was not totally up to scratch even though it had only covered 11,000 miles. It was not that anything was dramatically wrong, just that the steering was stiff, the clutch dragged, and the brakes needed too much pedal pressure. In the magazine's words, time and mileage had "reduced the controllability of the car below the potentialities of its engine". The engine itself, and the performance with which it endowed the car, came in for high praise.

This particular car had lost something over £800 in value during a little over two years. Its asking price of £1895 made it a tempting proposition for a buyer who might otherwise have been considering a more modestly priced new car. A Jaguar XK140

fixed-head coupé, for example, cost £1692 (including purchase tax), and some buyers might well have been tempted to take the two-year old Aston Martin instead. Even some relatively mundane models were not so much cheaper: a Riley Pathfinder for example – the Riley engine planted in a standard BMC body – was priced at £1411, and the Humber Super Snipe was £1426. On the other hand the secondhand Aston Martin needed work doing to bring it up to proper condition – although this might have been negotiated into the price – and would continue to need just as much regular attention as when it was new. Knowing that Aston Martin servicing was expensive anyway might have swayed a buyer back to a more boring but less financially risky new car.

Who would the lucky buyers have been who could afford a new DB2 and the servicing costs that went with it? In the early days, as we have seen, many of them were weekend racers who thought that the car represented a winning package. Then as now, racing required a deep pocket, so the DB2's price would not have been an obstacle in itself. As time went on, the car became more oriented towards the businessman with a family: the occasional seats were added, luggage space was extended, ventilation was improved. For those who wanted to go racing, the DB3 and DB3S were available, but the DB2 range were cars which could be used all day, every day. Those who chose

them were certainly members of an elite. Working on a rule of thumb that says people run a car worth about a third of their yearly income, these buyers would have been earning upwards of £7000 per annum, at a time when £10 a week was a good wage. Even run-of-the-mill company directors, earning £3-4000 per annum, were out of the Aston Martin league; if they were given a company car – and they probably were, even in those days – it might have been a Rover 75 or, later, a Jaguar 2.4.

Our typical DB2 buyer would have considered himself a cut above this level. Probably self-employed, or else at the top of a major company,

he might have justified the acquisition of a new Bentley, but would have felt that such a car gave him the wrong image. Possession of an Aston Martin DB2 showed the world that he was of a younger and less conservative disposition, and that although he was certainly wealthy he was less concerned about displaying his wealth. The Harley Street specialist, whose car Innes Ireland serviced, fits this profile exactly. Indeed, for the man in this position who wanted something a bit different there were very few alternatives, unless he spent a fortune on a foreign import. The successive models of Alvis and Bristol came the closest, but neither

"A very sporting car that you can drive in a dinner jacket" – DB2 on the 1958 RAC Rally.

had the sporting pedigree of the Aston Martin.

By the time the DB2 had developed into its final versions, the DB2/4 Mark II and Mark III, it occupied a unique position on the British market. Even the motoring press had difficulty describing its character. We have already met John Bolster's definition, "a very sporting car that you can drive in a dinner jacket". *The Motor* thought that the car deserved the title of "the world's fastest station wagon". The American *Road & Track* thought it was "a sleek, lithe vehicle, suitable for a race or a trip across town", while back in the UK *The Autocar* said that "a successful attempt has been made to combine the exhilaration of high-speed travel with the luxury of refined transport". All these ideas pointed towards the way the car was increasingly being used by its owners, namely for Continental travel.

Although petrol rationing had been abolished in 1950, foreign travel for British residents (other than on business) had been held back by exchange controls, whereby the amount of foreign currency which an individual could purchase in any one year was severely limited. Although this restriction was gradually eased, it was not until the late 1950s that a family, however well off, could consider a worthwhile touring holiday abroad. Once that became feasible, however, the fast Continental roads beckoned, just as they had before the war. An Aston Martin DB Mark III, with its four seats, large luggage capacity and outstanding performance, made the ideal vehicle, particularly if it was fitted with the newly-available overdrive. An *Autocar* road test summed it up: "Overdrive was appreciated on the Continent, where much of the testing took place; it made cruising between 80 and 100mph restful,

Continental touring the Aston Martin way.

almost to the point of seeming a leisurely form of travel, and the excellent siting of the switch enabled normal top to be regained in an instant".

Here, perhaps, we have the essential appeal of the DB2 series Aston Martins. Those who sought out-and-out performance had been taken care of by the DB3 and its successors, but the buyers who wanted to combine comfort with high-speed transportation were attracted more and more to the successive models of DB2 and DB2/4. They were looking essentially for a "grand touring" car, before the initials GT had ever been thought of, and the epitome of this type of travel was touring in Europe. No holiday thrill could come close to the sight of your car being swung on board the cross-channel ferry (no drive-on/ drive-off in those early postwar days) or, even better, to see it being driven up into the bowels of a Bristol Freighter belonging to Silver City Airways or Channel Air Bridge. The British, an island race, have always regarded the act of leaving their country as an intoxicating mixture of danger, pleasure and treason. Now, for those who could afford it, there was the ideal means of transport in which to indulge this feeling.

Chapter Nine

On the road now

If you have read this far and are not already an owner of a DB2 series car, you are probably seriously considering becoming one. Should you take the plunge? What are the pros and cons? How should you go about it?

Perhaps the most reassuring part of Aston Martin ownership is the knowledge that it is nowadays a continuing marque, firmly established and backed by a giant international group. It was not always like this; during the 1970s and 1980s, before the Ford takeover, there were serious doubts as to whether the name would survive. Today the posi-

Replacing a DB2/4's engine after reconditioning.

tion of Aston Martin in the marketplace is clear – it is an expensive but superbly-made high-performance car, challenging such makes as Porsche and Ferrari at the lower and upper limits of its price range. For the owner of a classic Aston, the upside is that there is a substantial population of existing cars and therefore a number of establishments competing to look after them. The downside is that the cars are sophisticated, complex and expensive, and so parts and labour rates also tend towards the expensive.

It is probably true to say, however, that the DB2 series is a less costly proposition than later models. This is because, in one of many moves to help the company's finances in difficult times, the rights to produce parts for all models up to and including the DB2/4 Mark III were franchised out to a third party, Aston Service Dorset. The Aston Martin company retained responsibility for parts supply for the DB4 onwards, and this is still the case today. Thus there tends to be an "inner circle" of service establishments specialising in the more modern cars, with close links to the factory; many of them are part of the company's Heritage Specialist Network, with the right to use the Heritage Mark. Outside this circle lie other specialists, working to just as high a standard in most cases, who tend to deal more with older cars and – inevitably, therefore – with restoration as well as service. For the DB2 range in particular, as well as Aston Service Dorset the other recognised specialists are the Moss family at Four Ashes Garage near Stratford-on-Avon.

A DB2/4 drophead coupé being serviced.

Parts for DB2s come primarily, as we have said, from Aston Service Dorset, but not all parts are available, and of course some are proprietary parts which are often stocked by other suppliers since they are used on a variety of makes. Examples of the latter are carburettors, where there are firms specialising in both SU and Weber parts, and electrical items, which were of Lucas manufacture and where a number of firms are able to supply replacement items. Where a newly-manufactured replacement simply does not exist, there is usually a well-developed secondhand market; for engine parts it is worth remembering that the 2.6- and 2.9-litre Lagonda units were virtually identical to their Aston Martin equivalents. As for repairs or restoration, it is usually a case of "you get what you pay for". By far the best recommendation is that of a knowledgeable friend who has used the firm in question for the type of work you want. Failing this, you could start by talking to your nearest Heritage dealer or local specialist. Remember that restoration costs, by the nature of the work, are virtually impossible to estimate accurately, and if you do manage to force even a rough estimate out of the firm's proprietor, the final cost is always higher. Nevertheless it helps to know what the hourly charging rate is, and then to keep a tally of hours worked against progress made; a reputable firm will put this in writing in the form of a monthly invoice.

So there is every chance that, if you decide to buy your DB2 or even DB3, you will not have a

*The interior of a
DB2 after
restoration.*

*Cutting out rusted
metal at the start of
a restoration.*

problem in obtaining spares, or in having any sort of work done on the car from a routine service to total restoration. But is it the sort of car you would enjoy owning and using in today's conditions? We have already seen how when it was new the car was admired for both its road behaviour and its performance. We have also learned that, while its performance by today's standards is less outstanding, it can still keep up with most modern traffic. As to roadholding, to avoid being embarrassed in wet conditions it might be wise to fit radial tyres in place of the original crossplies, but you should then use the enhanced grip with restraint so as not to over-stress the chassis. Importantly, which particular model would suit your needs best? Do you need the two occasional seats at the back which come with the DB2/4, or do you prefer the purer lines of the DB2? Or do you need an automatic gearbox, which only came with the DB2/4 Mark III?

Most important of all is the question of an open car or a closed one. The attractions of the drophead coupé are strong: most of us have a vision – fantasy, even – of reliving those perfect summers of our youth, when glamorous, upper-class couples spent their weekends driving their open Aston Martins into the countryside for picnics by the river. The reality, of course, is that – at least in Britain – a drophead will for obvious reasons spend the great majority of its time with its hood up, leaving back-seat passengers with no opportunity to see outside and take their minds off their discomfort. Nevertheless when the sun comes out and the hood gets folded away there is nothing to compare with the joys of open motoring. Regrettably it only comes at a price; with DB2s, as with virtually all classic cars, the open versions command a substantial premium. Bear in mind, too, that the saloon versions are if anything rarer than the open ones, and could therefore be said to represent something of a bargain. On the other hand if there is any question of major body repairs then this is an argument for choosing the drophead coupé, since the body panels will have to be removed from their frame and this is a slightly less drastic job than on the saloon.

There are a number of further decisions to take, and all of them will have an impact on what you might have to pay. First and foremost is whether to try for a "perfect" car (if such a thing exists), which has already been restored and will need no further work for a considerable time, or instead to find one which is fundamentally sound but which requires restoration to a greater or lesser degree. Each one of us has a different perspective on this question, strongly influenced by the funds we have available, and advice is probably unnecessary. While restoration costs are extremely difficult to estimate in advance, a restored car represents a firm and final cost (we hope!), particularly if it

Stripping a Mark III chassis.

Aston-Martin specialists handle a wide range of models. Here the DB4 prototype, DP 114/2, is approaching completion of its restoration at the works.

comes with a detailed photographic record. As against this, with a car whose restoration you have overseen yourself you can be reasonably certain that the work has been carried out satisfactorily. Furthermore, fully restored cars come on to the market only occasionally, and you may have to wait quite a time for the right one.

Once you have decided to embark on a purchase, the best move is always to join the relevant club, in this case the Aston Martin Owners Club. Founded in 1935, it has grown to become a thriving organisation with members all over the world and a permanent headquarters in a beautiful converted tithe barn in Oxfordshire. Their knowledge of all Aston Martin models is encyclopaedic, and they will usually be able to confirm the history of a particular car. The quarterly magazine and monthly news sheet are packed with good advice, and in the latter case with advertisements as well; this is an excellent place to start looking for a car, as they are often advertised there before the seller considers other channels. It is in the news sheet and on the Club website you will also find second-hand spares for sale. There are close and continuing relations between the Club and the

Aston Martin company.

The Club's headquarters building also houses the Aston Martin Heritage Trust. This was set up comparatively recently with the aim of preserving the company's history and the many artefacts associated with it – memorabilia, drawings, photographs, trophies and so on. The Trust even has its own historic cars: a 1921 Bamford & Martin (the oldest Aston Martin in existence), a 1935 Ulster model, an AMR1 Group C racer and a "Towns" Lagonda. Usually there are other models also on display in the barn, lent by members from time to time. The Club's archives are held there, and are invaluable in answering member's questions. As a charitable trust it opens its doors at specified times to members of the public, whereas AMOC members – who automatically become members of the Trust – can visit the headquarters during any normal business hours.

The advantage of being a member while you are still looking for a car is that you can use the Club's facilities to help you check on any candidates, and – as far as possible – to prevent your making an expensive mistake. It may well be, for example, that some of the experts amongst the membership can tell you more about a car's previous history than a dealer is able to (or wants to!). Whatever the car that interests you, make sure that an expert in the marque examines it for you. You will of course want to drive or be driven in the car, ideally the former. First, though – assuming the engine is not already hot – you should remove the radiator cap and inspect the condition of the coolant. Any suggestion of oil being mixed in is a warning of trouble. At minimum it could require a new water pump, but much more likely is a problem with the cylinder head gasket. The worst scenario is problems with the sealing of the wet liners, which effectively means an engine rebuild. When you get into the car, your first impression will be how low the floor seems, although this is mainly an illusion brought about by the need to climb over the high, wide sills, a legacy of the square-tube chassis. Once in, however, you will be pleasantly surprised by the comfortable seating position, and the accessibility of the controls. You will also probably notice the long bar under the instrument panel which opens the bonnet catch.

During your drive you will have checked the operation of the steering and brakes and listened to any suspicious noises – especially in the gearbox. An instrument check will have told you if

the all-important oil-pressure is satisfactory (ideally 50psi at 2500rpm when hot and certainly no less than 30psi), and will have checked such things as the charging rate and the working of the petrol gauge. It will also have helped if you have been able to examine the car from underneath, since the chassis can suffer from rust damage, particularly under each door where the cruciform bracing joins the sidemember. There are other known weak points, such as the steel sills on the later DB2/4s, corrosion of aluminium components in the suspension, and cracked blocks (particularly serious with the 2.6-litre engine, where repairs are not possible). It is here that an Aston specialist is so useful, since he will be aware of these points where others might not.

Another aspect of Club membership is the opportunity to take part in competitions, especially racing; it may be that your main reason for wanting to acquire a DB2 series car is to do exactly that. This section of the Club is very active and organises over a dozen events – race meetings, hill-climbs, speed events and track days – in a typical year. And this is in Britain alone; many Club members travel to European historic events each season as well. There are annual trophies for different groups of models, including one for the

Oxfordshire headquarters of the Aston Martin Owners' Club and the Heritage Trust.

Former works car LML/50/50 taking part in a historic sports-car race at Donington.

"Feltham" cars. Alternatively one can enter less stressful events such as concours d'elegance, and these are often combined with social events such as weekend breaks.

An important attraction to many owners of 1950s Aston Martins is the opportunity to enjoy driving their car as part of a holiday, such as on a Continental tour. In many ways touring is an ideal way of using such a car, since it allows you to become much more familiar with it than just by taking it out for a day trip or even a weekend. And to do so on the less busy roads of continental Europe is even more of a pleasure, not just because the

weather is likely to be better – and surely that is reason enough – but also because the lower traffic density in most European countries makes driving much less of a strain. There are many times even now, on the minor roads of, say, central or south-west France, where you can imagine yourself back in the 1950s, taking the family down to Biarritz in your brand-new Aston Martin without a care in the world and without the hordes of modern cars that so easily spoil the illusion in crowded Britain.

The DB2/4 was singled out at the time for its suitability for long-distance touring. The luggage capacity, in particular, was considered vast, and it

is still more than adequate today, especially if only two of you are going to tour and you can use the rear seat space as well. This is not to say that they cannot take four people and their luggage, provided the rear two passengers are on the small side. The only note of caution is that on the saloon there is no provision, as there is nowadays in estate cars, for a roller blind to protect the luggage from prying eyes, so you should take extra care in choosing where you park.

Needless to say you would not embark on such a trip unless you had confidence in the reliability of your car. This is a good reason to work up your

new car to a long tour via a number of shorter ones within closer range of home, where the consequences of a breakdown are less serious. Partly, too, your confidence will depend on your mechanical knowledge and experience. If you have misgivings on this point, you will no doubt begin by touring in the company of other like-minded owners. In this respect the AMOC can once again be of help, since every year they organise tours for members, either within Europe or further afield. However, once you become more confident you and a few friends can start to make your own arrangements, with a timetable to suit yourselves.

A DB2/4 leads a DB2 in a race at Brands Hatch.

Historic sports-car racing is equally popular in North America. Taking part here is a former works car, DB3S/10.

These days breakdown insurance cover is not only more affordable but also much more comprehensive than years ago, so the consequences of even a serious malfunction are less disastrous: your car is transported home, a hire car is put at your disposal and you continue with your holiday. Of course not every such breakdown service is prepared to cover older cars outside the United Kingdom, and this is yet another area where the Club can probably point you in the right direction.

When you go on a long tour you should not forget the grease-gun, since the king-pins will need greasing after 1000 miles. Fortunately the remaining 14 grease points can last for intervals of 2500 miles, and this is probably as much mileage as most of these cars will cover in a year nowadays. At the same time the engine oil will need changing, but again to do this every year regardless of mileage is recommended treatment for a classic car. The DB2 series is of course one of the easier models to work on with its fully-opening, one-piece bonnet – a feature copied nearly 10 years later by the Triumph Herald. The ease of access which this gives to both engine and front suspension is a revelation, and it makes minor maintenance such as lubrication or brake adjust-ment almost a pleasure. However, only the dedicated amateur engineer will be prepared to undertake the more complex tasks, and most owners will happily leave these to an Aston Martin specialist.

There is no need to regard your DB2 as only a summer weekend car, and there are plenty of owners who use theirs all the year round. If you do put your car away for winter you should remember that it is damp rather than cold that is the enemy, and an investment in a dehumidifier could be well worthwhile. Even if you do take the car out occasionally during the winter you should notice that it starts fairly easily because it has not suffered dampness in the engine compartment which can play havoc with the HT side of the ignition. Dehumidifiers are comparatively inexpensive these days, and they have the additional benefit of providing you with a source of distilled water which you can use in the battery, radiator (with anti-freeze added) or steam-iron.

If you intend to use your chosen car primarily for competition work, you will no doubt first put all the mechanical parts through a complete inspection and refurbishment – and replace them with new ones where there is the slightest doubt.

When not competing on race-tracks, Aston Martin owners are often to be found at a concours d'elegance.

This is essential where 50 year old parts are going to be stressed near the limits for which they were originally designed and made. If, however, you intend to confine yourself to touring and normal road use, such stringent measures are probably unnecessary. All that is necessary is that you make some allowance for the car's long life and the subtle metallurgical changes which may have taken place during that time. This means, for example, not using the full revolutions available from the engine: imposing a limit of, say, 3500rpm on your-self rather than the original 5000rpm will approximately halve the stress on the big-end and main bearings. It will also help if you avoid cruising at a constant speed on the motorway, since such conditions were virtually unheard of when the car was new and the engine's lubrication system was not designed for them. Instead, every mile or so just let up on the throttle for a couple of seconds. This will ensure two things: firstly the crankshaft bearings, particularly the big-ends,will shift their contact points and allow the oil film to re-establish itself, and secondly oil will be sucked

There's plenty of work left to do before this MkIII is back on the road, but it will certainly be worth it.

down into the valve guides.

This also brings up the thorny question of unleaded petrol and its effect on the valve seats. You will find plenty of advice from the Club's experts, but in general it is not necessary in normal use to modify these engines by fitting hardened inserts, since the particular type of cast iron used actually hardens over time. Moreover with the later engines, such as the Mark III's, with larger valves, there is little room left for the necessary machining. If you live near one of the outlets which has continued to sell leaded petrol you may decide to do nothing. On the other hand you may want to add one of the several additives to your petrol which are sold as substitutes for the effect of tetraethyl lead.

Whichever direction you decide to go with your DB2 – track events, concours d'elegance, touring in the UK or on the Continent, or just driving out to a pub – you will be sure to find like-minded Aston Martin owners with similar interests. May your new acquisition and your new friends bring you many hours of pleasure!

ROAD TEST DATA

Type	Year	Model	Price (basic) £	Weight lb	Brake at 30 mph %	Acceleration 0-60 mph Sec	0-100 mph Sec	Top Max Mph	Top Mean Mph	Fuel Cons'n Mpg	Comments
DB2	1950	saloon	1598	2450	89	11.2	34.5	117.3	116.4	20	'Motor' 27.9.50 – Vantage engine
DB2	1951	dhc	1598	2460		12.7		109		20	'Motor Sport' Feb '51
DB2	1951	saloon		2460		10.8		122			'Mechanix Illustrated' (US) Jul '51
DB2	1951	saloon		2500		11.9	36	109	105.7		'Road & Track' (US) Dec '51
DB2/4	1953	saloon	1850	2730	83	12.6	40.4	120	111	20.3	'Autocar' 2.10.53
DB2/4	1954	saloon	1850	2630	100	10.9	35.6	117.8	114.6	19.4	'Top Gear' May '54
DB2/4	1954	saloon	1850	2730	90	10.5	30.0	120.3	118.5	23.0	'Motor' 25.8.54
DB2/4	1954	saloon	1925	2740	79	11.1	31.7	120.0	118.7	20.1	'Autocar' 3.9.54
DB2/4 Mk II	1955	saloon	1925	2630		10.0	27.0	120.9	119.2	20	'Autocourse' May '55
DB3S	1956	open sports	2600	2185		6.6	14.4	140.6		10	'Autosport' 10.2.56
DB2/4 Mk II	1957	saloon	1925	2690		10.0	28.0	118.4		23	'Autosport' 31.5.57
DB Mk III	1957	saloon	2050	2900	85	9.3	31.0	120	119	18.1	'Autocar' 27.12.57
DB Mk III	1958	saloon		2950		9	33	120	118		'Road & Track' (US) Dec '58
DB Mk III	1959	saloon	2050	2885		8.2	23.8				'Autocourse' Jan '59 – 4.09:1 axle

CHASSIS NUMBERS

Model	Dates	Starts at	Finishes at	Comments
Two-Litre Sports (DB1)	Sept '48 – May '50	AMC/48/1	AMC/50/15	LMA/48/1 was SPA/48/1
DB2	May '50 – Apr '53	LMA/49/1	LML/50/406	Change from A to L indicates Lagonda (6-cyl) engine
		LML/50/X1	LML/50/X5	Reason for X suffix unknown
DB2/4	Oct '53 – Oct '55	LML/501	LML/1065	
DB2/4 Mk II	Oct '55 – Aug '57	AM300/1101	AM300/1299	
DB Mk III	Mar '57 – July '59	AM300/3A/1300	AM300/3/1850	'A' prefix indicated disc brake option on first 100 cars
DB3	Sept '51 - May '53	DB3/1	DB3/10	
DB3S	1953 – 1956	DB3S/1	DB3S/11	Works cars only
		DB3S/101	DB3S/120	

Index